Regaining a nation: equality and democracy

John Robinson

This book is sold subject to the condition that it will not, by way of trade or otherwise, be re-sold, hired out or otherwise circulated without the publisher's prior written consent, in any form of binding or cover other than that in which it is published and without a similar condition, including this condition, being imposed on the subsequent purchaser. No part of this book may be reproduced by any process, stored in a retrieval system, or transmitted in any form without the prior permission of the publisher.

Copyright 2022 John Robinson

ISBN 9781872970 85 0

Published by Tross Publishing,
P.O. Box 22 143,
Khandallah,
Wellington 6441
New Zealand.

Printed by Your Books,
18 Cashew Street,
Grenada North,
Wellington

Cover design: Clark design
clarkdesign@xtra.co.nz

For other Tross Publishing books see:
www.trosspublishing.co.nz

All doctrines, policies and practices based on or advocating superiority of peoples or individuals on the basis of national origin or racial, religious, ethnic or cultural differences are racist, scientifically false, legally invalid, morally condemnable and socially unjust.
United Nations Declaration on the Rights of Indigenous Peoples 2007, Introduction.

I have a dream that my four little children will one day live in a nation where they will not be judged by the colour of their skin but by the content of their character.
Martin Luther King, August 28, 1963, at the Lincoln Memorial during the March on Washington for Jobs and Freedom

Dr John Robinson is a scientist with a PhD degree from the Massachusetts Institute of Technology. He has described the story of the early days of New Zealand in a series of books, from *Unrestrained Slaughter; the Maori Musket Wars 1800-40* **to** *The Kingite Rebellion,* **followed by a consideration of culture and recent developments, as in** *Dividing a nation; the return to tikanga* **and his classic work,** *He Puapua; Blueprint for breaking up New Zealand.*

Contents

Introduction 6
Crisis 2022: Apartheid New Zealand 11
PART 1: CELEBRATING COLONISATION 15
    Before Maori: the first settlers 15
    Early nineteenth century war and social breakdown 21
    Cultural transformation, the new Maori society 27
    The real Treaty of Waitangi 31
    Peace agreements, Auckland, around 1840 35
    Freeing slaves, Waikato 1842 40
    Great meeting of chiefs, Kohimarama 1860 48
    Peace celebration at Waitara, 1878 51
    Sir Apirana Ngata at the centennial celebration of 1940 62
    Challenges faced; difficulties overcome 69
    Progress through the twentieth century 73
PART 2: BUILDING A NATION 80
    Whaling, sealing, timber and construction industries 80
    Missionaries, settlers and farmers 86
    Roads and rail 90
    Wool and meat 95
    Home comforts 97
    Schools, health care, and housing 100
    Science and knowledge 110
    A proud story 118

PART 3: DESTROYING DEMOCRACY 120
   The Waitangi Tribunal 120
   Destruction of the Treaty of Waitangi 130
   A nation divided 137
   Rewriting history and redefinition of racism 141
   The end of freedom of speech 148
   A ruthless ideology 159
   Tribalism triumphant: the *He Puapua* tsunami 173
   Co-governance – constitutional transformation based on race.. 178
   An existing separate Maori government 186
   Apartheid in practice 196
PART 4: RECOVERY 202
   The good life: equality and democracy 202
   The great challenge ahead 209
   Major policies 214
   Combined action 218
   Bibliography 227
   Index 233

Introduction

Our country, New Zealand, the place where we live, is in deep trouble. It is time to stop and think, to look across the whole picture, and to recognise how far the idea of community has been ripped apart.

Following two introductory chapters, this book is divided into in four sections.

'Celebrating colonisation' commences the story with the first coming of people to New Zealand, to be followed by the canoes bringing the ancestors of the several present-day Maori *iwi*, when the indigenous *tangata whenua* were slaughtered and driven away from their settlements.

Fighting among the tribes in the first several decades of the nineteenth century, with many battles across the country, with massacres and ethnic cleansing, and with conflict expanded by movements of large bands of refugees, brought social breakdown and a rapid population decline.

Many Maori were distressed by the anarchy and social collapse. Their calls for help from the British were answered by the Treaty of Waitangi, giving sovereignty to the British Crown and equal citizenship to all New Zealanders.

The welcoming of a national government was a key element of the comprehensive Maori cultural transformation when most turned away from the previous precepts of *tikanga* to Christianity. There were great meetings and peace-making between the previously fighting tribes, and slaves were set free to return to their former homes.

When, a few decades later, a few raised the banners of revolt and threatened to overturn the government, many chiefs gathered (at the

Kohimarama Conference) to celebrate and support the colonisation that had brought peace and development.

After the fighting ended, several former rebels (such as Rewi Maniapoto) worked with the government, becoming close friends and celebrating the return of peace. At the 1940 Centennial celebrations Sir Apirana Ngata recognised the advances of the century following colonisation: "That is the outstanding fact today, that but for the seal of the sovereignty handed over to Her Majesty and her descendants I doubt that there would be a free Maori race in New Zealand today."[1]

The **'Building a nation'** section shows how New Zealand was built by many people, adapting Western science and knowhow to local conditions. Trade in seals, whales, flax and timber had commenced before 1840, with the active involvement of many Maori. There followed the development of farming, the building of roads and railways, and the growth of industry, most notably in wool and meat.

While many Maori took part in the development of a modern nation, others had continued to live apart until the availability of jobs brought a migration into the cities during and following the Second World War – when they gained better access to health care and education, and many social measures (which had certainly got much better after 1840, but which still lagged behind those of other New Zealanders) improved as they became further integrated into the developed economy.

Many Maori had become part of the working class and they suffered disproportionately by the considerable increase in inequality due to the emphasis on the market and globalisation after 1984, which had no relation to the former colonisation period that was long past.

That class experience has been wrongly attributed to supposed wrongs of colonisation, resulting in a Maori movement away from a

---

[1] Ngata 1940

national identity with the aim of **'Destroying democracy'** to set up a divided society, with a dual government giving disproportionate power to the race-based Maori minority of the tribal elite.

This has involved a considerable effort over many years, building a considerable organisation and making inroads into many aspects of government. After a lengthy time of gestation and formation, the overthrow of the Westminster form of government has gained speed and expanded to build up a commanding influence in recent years. Such is the rapidity of events that my 2021 book *He Puapua* required two updates in just a few months; a full record would require at least a full new book each year to keep up with the massive and fundamental destruction of our way of life and the ongoing transformation to complete separation of two declared races.

It is important here to remind ourselves of the requirement for equality in a genuine democracy, to appreciate the evolution of a decent and fair way of life where we can all live together with respect for us all and no domination by any one group.

There is much to celebrate in the story of New Zealand but this has been denied by 'revisionist' historians. The false narrative of past wrongs has led to a redefinition of racism, so that opposition to inequality and the 'positive discrimination' which provides special rights to a racial group is now said to be 'racist'. The pot calls the kettle black. This has resulted in a denial of freedom of speech (a supposed 'human right') to those who insist on holding to the well-established ideal of equality, as well as in the reinterpretation, indeed reinvention, of the Treaty of Waitangi, resulting in the application of a completely different (and unclear) new version in law while the captured media are now required to follow the directives of the revised Treaty.

There are now many references to specific Maori rights and power in legislation and government services, supported by the activities of the divisive Waitangi Tribunal, 47 years old and still going strong, even expanding in power. Co-governance is leading towards the declared goal of a racially separated dual system of government with two houses of parliament. The narrative is tightly controlled and critics are firmly exiled to the side-lines.

The Helen Clark government had drawn a line in the sand and made it clear that there would be no division of the nation by race, with its 2004 Foreshore and Seabed Act and a refusal to sign up to the 2007 United Nations Declaration on the Rights of Indigenous Peoples (UNDRIP) with its many special rights to 'indigenous' people. But this principle was smashed by the John Key National government which wrote that division into law with its 2011 Marine and Coastal Area Act and then signed up to UNDRIP. Those changes (contrary to previous policies of both the National and Labour Parties) were readily accepted by the current Jacinda Ardern Labour government which has moved further down that divisive path with division of many more aspects of government and a move to co-governance, following the directions of a constitutional transformation as set down in the *He Puapua* report to government (itself based on the *Iwi Leaders Forum* report *Matike Mai Aotearoa)*. The two main parties have shown that they cannot be trusted to protect equality and unity.

In the face of this existential challenge, New Zealand needs to fight back and move to a process of **'Recovery'**, to once again hold firm to the proclamation that **we are one people**. This search for a better future must be based on a common belief in what makes a good life for us all – a society governed by principles of equality and democracy. The country has moved far from any such ideals, and there will be a considerable struggle, a true counter-revolution, before that goal can be reached. It is not difficult to set down a list of policies leading in the required direction, but not so easy to set down a plan of action. Many people have tried, and are working hard now, but the juggernaut, the tsunami, is rolling on. Only united action will succeed.

In May, 2022, political commentator Chris Trotter wrote[2]:

"What began as an anti-co-governance narrative, and then merged with an anti-mainstream news media narrative, risks joining with a much older and more deeply entrenched narrative concerning the entire Treaty settlement process. This is the narrative that identifies the primary beneficiaries of Treaty settlements as a collection of Crown-assembled tribal elites, along with their legal and commercial advisers. Over the past thirty years these 'Neo-Tribal Capitalists' have been accused of investing hundreds-of-millions of taxpayer dollars in what amount to private tribal corporations, over which the intended recipients of these funds – *hapu* and *whanau* – exercise only the most indirect authority and receive only the most meagre of rewards.

The result could very easily be the emergence of what might be called a 'super-narrative' in which all the negatives of co-governance, media capture, and Neo-Tribal Capitalism are rolled into one big story about the deliberate corruption of New Zealand democracy. The guilty parties would be an unholy alliance of *Pakeha* and Maori elites determined to keep public money flowing upwards into protected private hands. In this super-narrative, the structures set forth in *He Puapua* to secure *tino rangatiratanga*, will actually ensure the exclusion of the vast majority of New Zealanders from the key locations of power, the only positive consequence of which will be a common struggle for political and economic equality in which non-elite Maori and *Pakeha* will have every incentive to involve themselves."

Here is one such narrative. That common struggle for equality is long overdue.

---

[2] https://thedailyblog.co.nz/2022/05/31/must-read-nanaias-super-narrative/

Crisis 2022: Apartheid New Zealand

There is a new madness afoot. This is not the country I grew up in, a place of democracy, equality and fair play for all, with none bowing down to the pre-eminence of any proclaimed special group.

The New Zealand government is carrying out a constitutional transformation, bedding in a system of racial inequality and carrying out the complete destruction of our democracy in a self-inflicted national catastrophe. This is no longer a unified nation of equal citizens.

A determined race-based minority, within the Maori community, is seizing control of the country, while most others remain ill-informed, unaware and uncaring. Many in positions of power are following the new divisive ideology, building careers by adherence to the new orthodoxy, remaining ignorant or uncaring of the consequences. Those who are aware of the destruction of a way of life are blocked from speaking out by a subservient media, which is funded by government to follow the required ideology.

The division is well advanced and has powerful supporters, moving steadily towards the proclaimed joint rule of two parliaments planned for 2040 – a race-based system of government with unequal rights – New Zealand apartheid.

Co-governance has become a recognised policy option, and it is in place in many actions across the country (some examples are noted in the chapter on Co-governance). The process of division by race and vastly unequal representation that has been building for several decades went into full-speed-ahead high gear in 2021, and continues at top speed in 2022, galloping along unchecked towards the ultimate goal of complete apartheid, with two separate governments defined by race.

The concept of rule by a special group, defined by class or race or military might, based on a former seizure of power is long gone from modern democracies – the idea of equality at birth has been fought for in many struggles over centuries until it has become a guide to modern societies. There is no more rule by aristocracy in Europe, or by a race-based regime in South Africa. New Zealand is taking a great leap backwards to a dark past of inherited inequality.

This ideology, this new orthodoxy, is based on a rewritten story of the past ('revisionist' history) that presents a false picture of wrongs of colonisation. That, and the offer of massive payments to *iwi* for Treaty of Waitangi claims, has served to build a sense of grievance among Maori, and a feeling of inherited guilt in others, providing a basis for an extreme form of 'positive discrimination' and special rights to Maori, who are wrongly defined as a 'race'.

A careful study of the facts provides a very different picture, indeed the very opposite. A correction of the whole distorted narrative is essential. Then we can all consider actions to return to equality and democracy, in a decent and fair country, respecting the interest of all citizens, with no longer a race bar.

My own feelings were set out clearly in an opening chapter, of my book *Dividing a Nation; the Return to tikanga*:[3]

"I am a New Zealander. I would like to have the same rights as every other citizen.

I grew up and spent my early adult years in a world fighting against the evils of apartheid in South Africa and racial discrimination in the southern United States of America. We all came to know of the injustices of those systems, and to abhor the division of people by the idea of race.

Now here in New Zealand we are divided, separated into two people – Maori and the rest. The division is made clear in much legislation,

---

[3] Robinson 2019

based on the definition of Maori as 'a person of the Maori race'. There it is, 'race' stated clearly as the basis of the division, as a bulwark of New Zealand law.

I cry for my beloved country.[4] We deserve something better, to be one people, with a land that belongs to all of us equally, all respected with our various ways and beliefs, none set above."

What is it that we want, now and for the future? We should not be held captive by the past. We have the right to make our own choice, the duty to future generations to hand them a well-functioning nation.

A better vision, which was that of previous generations of New Zealanders, is for equality and togetherness. Not division, separation and partnership between two race-defined peoples, with very unequal powers and rights.

The recovery of equality, decency, democracy involves the consideration of options and a call for action. First, we must recognise the importance of equality and the need for all New Zealanders to feel that they belong as one people in a united nation. Then to understand that an unchecked government in a one-house parliament, almost unique in the developed world, has allowed a powerful few to seize effective control of our country – the fundamental requirement for checks and balances on unbridled power is lacking.

Politicians of all parties have failed us, choosing to hold to power rather than to face and speak out against the growing division. While the challenge must be taken to the politicians, we would be foolish to trust and rely on them; those elected to both national and local body governments are far too subservient, the majority being content to 'go with the flow'.

---

[4] cribbed from Alan Paton, *Cry, the beloved country*, where he refers to apartheid South Africa

There is a spirit of idealism in each of us; we must awaken the spirit of personal freedom and responsibility, and take up the struggle; to learn more of the facts, to gain an understanding of the crisis and keep abreast of the increasing divisions and to join those who are active in the fight for equality and democracy – of all political persuasions – and build an effective counter-revolution force against the revolutionary tribal takeover of our country.

PART 1: CELEBRATING COLONISATION

Before Maori: the first settlers

While civilisations developed across the Eurasian continent, New Zealand remained uninhabited by man, being the last significant inhabitable landmass on earth to be discovered and settled. People first came to the Pacific Ocean around 4,000 years ago, having moved away from the Asian mainland and nearby islands thousands of years before that. They moved steadily from the north-west fringes of the Ocean, over several millennia, from island to island in a series of migrations, to colonise those many, different islands.

They came with the culture of the tribal societies of that past time, and remained frozen in time; there were no longer any direct connections with the mass of humanity across the Eurasian continent. They were separated from those many societies that developed through the Bronze Age (2300–700 BC) and the Iron Age (700–1 BC), as civilisations flourished, as understanding in philosophy, science, medicine evolved, and several great religions appeared. They did not share in the rich development of those civilisations elsewhere, with the many advances such as the use of metals, as well as writing, mathematics and systems of law. While the majority of peoples had been changing, evolving, developing in great ways, the Polynesians were isolated, wandering the Pacific and adjusting to local conditions with the tools at their disposal – hunter-gatherers with rudimentary agriculture and gardening and no large animals, without metals or the wheel, and preserving an ancient tribal structure.[5]

The first sign of the coming of people to New Zealand is evidence of rats living here. In 1996 scientist Richard Holdaway obtained 15 Pacific rat dates, by radiocarbon dating, with some rat bones at up to nearly 2,000 years of age (50–150 AD).[6] However, Holdaway assumed that these bones do not provide adequate information to establish settlement: "On the two main islands, radiocarbon dates on rat bones from natural sites show that rat populations were established more than 1,000 years before permanent human settlement, presumably during transient visits by Polynesian voyagers. ... Human assistance is needed for the establishment of a population of rats on a remote island. However, neither the arrival of humans accompanied by rats, nor the occupation of an island by humans who maintained contact with rat source areas, necessarily resulted in the establishment of a self-sustaining population of rats on that island."[7] We just don't know.

A number of geological studies and archaeological digs across the country provide evidence of early settlement, possibly as much as one thousand years before the coming of the Maori.[8] A 1952 paper on "Geological Evidence of the Antiquity of Man in the New Zealand Area" by G. L. Adkin of Geological Survey[9] summarises some of this evidence. "The findings of archaeology and tradition supplementary to the geological evidence and suggesting a scheme of successive migrations to the New Zealand region ... there is evidence of three separate and variant native cultures having been brought to and spread through these islands.

---

[5] Howe 2003, page 70; Robinson 2015, page 10; Robinson 2019, pages 73-76
[6] Holdaway 1996
[7] Holdaway 1999
[8] Robinson 2021, Appendix, 'Evidence from archaeology'
[9] Adkin 1952

(1) The Waitaha ... a people of superior material culture, Polynesian, culturally archaic.

(2) The Ngatimamoe, a people apparently largely Polynesian but with a possible Melanesian quality.

(3) The Fleet or Hawaiki Maori, a people predominantly Polynesian, but also possessing traits of culture and practice said to be unknown in oceanic Polynesia."

Adkin notes the possibility of settlement dates far before the then commonly accepted date of 1000 A.D., and the resulting uncertainty. Thus, "the incoming date of the Waitaha (put at 1,300 years earlier, around 300 B.C.) is open to the objection that this seems too lengthy a period for their sojourn in Horowhenua [Adkin's study had been in the Levin area], but apart from this a very much earlier date for them than has hitherto been attached to human immigrants to this country has much to warrant it."

Very substantial archaeological digs by T Russell Price over some 25 years at Poukawa in the Hawkes Bay region also provided evidence of human presence some thousands of years ago, with dating both from layers identifying well-dated eruptions, and from carbon dating.[10]

The results of this careful and professional research deserve further attention. Unfortunately, further research is blocked, as in the Northland Waipoua forest, where archaeologists have made detailed notes on stone walls, hearths, altars, obelisks, rock carvings, standing stone circles, circular stone mounds and stone lined waterways, and taken samples for carbon dating. In 1983, a group of archaeologists from Auckland University were employed by the then NZ Forest Service to investigate and document these structures, but in 1988 the archaeological records were transferred from Kaikohe to the National Archives in Wellington, with a 75-year embargo on the records,

---

[10] Doutré, undated

demanded by Te Rorora *iwi* and agreed to by the Department of Conservation (DOC).[11] There is much hidden here; the artefacts are clearly there.

A number of archaeological digs have produced evidence of early settlement, which demand further research by independent scientists to determine the full and fascinating story of our land. This is a puzzle demanding a solution but, since this is a challenge to the Maori claim of indigenous status, further work is not carried out and information is kept out of sight.

Many Maori described tales of prior settlers that are part of their tribal history. In the early twentieth century Maori doctor, Member of Parliament, visiting Professor of Anthropology at Yale University and Director of the Bishop Museum in Hawaii, Sir Peter Buck (Te Rangi Horoa) talked with many fellow Maori and travelled widely to small Pacific communities.[12] As a result of his considerable research, he identified three settlement periods.

It is generally recognised that the first discoverer was Kupe, although some traditional evidence suggests a previous discovery by an earlier group led by Maui, with "the Maui nation" in occupation before Kupe's voyage.

The first settlement period (apart from the possible 'Maui nation') was by three canoes (Kahutara, Taikoria and Okoki, commanded by Manuiwi, Ruatamori and Taitawaro) with the settlers referred to by Buck as "the *tangata whenua*", the first or indigenous people. They occupied territories along the west coast of the North Island, and soon "increased in numbers". Some subsequently moved to the south, including early tribes of the South Island, Waitaha and Rapuwai (later replaced by Ngati Mamoe and then Ngaitahu). Buck suggested that the Moriori of the Chatham Islands may have been descended from these first immigrants. There are a number of reports of the peaceful

---

[11] Waikanae Watch, June 10, 2021
[12] Buck 1949, pages 4-64; Robinson 2019, pages 78-84

lives of the *tangata whenua*[13], and of the later lack of resistance of the Moriori when they were conquered and massacred by Ngati Mutunga in 1835.

"The second influx of settlers to New Zealand is associated primarily with Toi, one of the most widely known names in early Maori history."[14] A number of voyaging canoes came, bringing settlers. They found people living here; Buck suggests that "they were numerous".

There were a number of conflicts between the first people and the newcomers, with *tangata whenua* being killed by Manaia so that the newcomers could possess the land.[15] "After the arrival of Toi and Whatonga from Eastern Polynesia, inter-marriages took place between the two migrations, and in the times of Awa-nui-a-rangi (circa 1200 [according to Buck]) wars of extermination commenced, ending in the practical extinction of the men of the *tangata-whenua*, whilst the women and children were absorbed by the conquerors."[16]

The third settlement period is the best known (Buck calls it "the most famous event in Maori history"), the coming of seven famous canoes, Tainui, Te Arawa, Matatua, Kurahaupo, Tokomaru, Aotea and Takitimu.

Many accounts suggest that the newcomers were advanced, warlike, agricultural tribes who destroyed or drove out the previous settlers, the first comers, including the Waitaha and the Moriori, and chased them away from their lands, following bloody battles.

While it has been proposed that settlement may have begun in the period AD 0-500 (based on information including that summarised above), the consensus that formed during the 20th century was of a

---

[13] Smith 1910, page 22
[14] Buck 1949, pages 22-35
[15] Smith 1910, page 34
[16] Smith 1910, Preface

date of around AD 800 for first colonisation, and the coming of Maori around AD 1300.

The best available information is unambiguous. Maori were not the first people to settle New Zealand. They were not indigenous, not the *tangata whenua.* **And their treatment of those they found living on the land was brutal, as they killed most men, took women as partners, and drove survivors away from settled regions – a behaviour that stands in marked contrast to the coming of peace with the arrival of the British.**

Early nineteenth century war and social breakdown

Pre-contact Maori lived in a tribal, warlike society. On his visit, in 1769, James Cook saw the fortified *pa* on many hilltops, and noted the considerable impact of warfare on Maori tribes, who "must live under perpetual apprehension of being destroyed by each other."[17] He later met natives who were afraid to travel from one bay to the next for fear of being killed and eaten, and heard stories of recent great battles.

A population decline may have been under way. "The natives attribute their decrease in numbers, before the arrival of the Europeans, to war and sickness, disease probably arising from the destruction of food and the forced neglect of cultivation caused by the constant and furious wars which devastated the country for a long period before the arrival of the Europeans, in such a manner that the natives at last believed that a constant state of warfare was the natural condition of life, and their sentiments, feelings, and maxims became gradually formed on this belief. Nothing was so valuable or respectable as strength and courage, and to acquire property by war and plunder was more honourable and also more desirable than by labour. Cannibalism was glorious. The island was a pandemonium."[18]

The extent of the widespread fighting was evident in the first two five-year periods of the nineteenth century, before the onset of the 'musket wars'. There were 23 significant battles with 2,300 casualties (probable deaths) in 1801-1805, 30 battles with 2,600 casualties in 1806-1810.[19]

---

[17] Wilson 1985, page 174; Robinson 2012, page 38
[18] Maning 1887, page 205; Robinson 2012, pages 40-41
[19] Rutherford, undated

Fighting increased considerably in 1816-1820, to 122 battles with 6,900 casualties and mushroomed out further after Hongi Hika returned from England with his many muskets purchased using the proceeds of the gifts he had been given – to 203 battles (one significant battle each nine days across the country!), with 14,800 casualties, in 1821-1825.

The population could not support that level of mortality, and female infanticide made significant further inroads into the 'breeding stock' so that there was insufficient replacement for even a normal level of mortality. An estimate is that the Maori population fell from 137,600 in 1800 to 71,600 in 1840 (a drop of 48%), guaranteeing a further population decline for decades to come, until the peace and security of colonisation brought recovery, and population growth after 1890.[20]

There was fighting across the entire country, as refugees escaping the fighting spread the carnage. For example, Ngati Toa under Te Rauparaha (with their allies Te Atiawa, Ngati Raukawa, Ngati Tama) escaped the genocide by Waikato to Kapiti, where they repeated the pattern by killing and driving out the people of that land (including Muaupoko, Rangitane, Ngati Apa, Ngati Ira and Ngati Kahungunu), before continuing with murderous attacks on Wellington and the South Island. One further ally, Ngati Mutunga, helped defeat the inhabitants of Wellington before continuing to destroy the Moriori of the Chatham Islands.[21]

The wartime alliance of Ngati Haua, Waikato, Ngati Maniapoto and Ngaiterangi formed by the warrior chief Waharoa during the musket wars was later to provide the base for the king movement, led by his son, Wiremu Tamihana Tarapipipi Te Waharoa (William Thompson), which in the 1860s was to fight against the government for a separate state.[22]

---

[20] Robinson 2015, page 310
[21] Robinson 2020
[22] Robinson 2020, page 58

The disruption of war, with populations killed off or moving away from harm left much productive land bare, as in Auckland, the Tamaki isthmus, a land rich in natural resources, with fertile soil and plentiful seafood from both the Waitemata and Manukau Harbours.

The first tribal settlements there had followed the same pattern as across much of New Zealand, as many of the original people were killed or absorbed by conquering tribes. The most important group of the circa 1350 canoes (those people who came to known as Maori) was Tainui, some of whose people intermarried with local people to found the Ngai Tai tribe.[23]

Over the following centuries there were periods of calm, broken by attacks by various war parties. By the seventeenth century, the two main tribes in the Auckland area were Ngaiwi and Waiohua, and Ngati Paoa (from Hauraki) also had become a formidable presence in Tamaki.[24] In the eighteenth century, Ngati Whatua came from the north (around Kaipara) and conquered the Waiohua *iwi*, around 1750. This was a common route for many large war-parties, the scene of many battles. "Over the next eighty years, Tamaki's population remained relatively small, a fraction of what it had been. Settlement and cultivation no longer covered much of the isthmus."[25]

In 1819, a powerful *taua* of Ngapuhi and Ngati Whatua from the north passed through (and attacked Waikato and Ngati Paoa food-gathering parties, with cannibal feasts near Parnell and the Auckland Domain) on their way to join Ngati Toa and continuing to spread destruction as far south as Wellington.

In 1821, a Ngapuhi army of two thousand men led by Hongi Hika, half with muskets, assembled in the Bay of Islands, before setting off in around fifty canoes, each carrying up to fifty men. The *taua* attacked and defeated the Mokoia *pa*, on the northern side of the

---

[23] Stone 2001, page 13
[24] Stone 2001, pages 19 and 23
[25] Stone 2001, pages 47-48

Panmure Basin; all within were killed and the *taua* feasted on the bodies until the stench of putrefaction drove them on. They then turned to a second Ngati Paoa *pa*, Mauinaina, where the slaughter was even greater, with claims that over one thousand were killed.

In 1824, there was another great Ngapuhi campaign against Ngati Whatua. When the Ngati Whatua force advanced to the attack, and the two great *taua* faced one another across gentle country covered with ferns, Hongi Hika ordered his forces to fire concentrated musket volleys. Ngati Whatua were again cut down by the massed Ngapuhi muskets, and large numbers of slaves were taken back to the Bay of Islands, many to serve as food or as goods for trade.[26]

In 1820, Rev. John Butler and Rev. Samuel Marsden had seen fertile gardens there, with around twenty villages; but in 1833 the Tamaki isthmus was a man-made desert – Rev. Henry Williams had seen that the land was overgrown and no sign of an inhabitant could be seen in any direction.[27] The number of passing *taua* had reduced the area to an almost empty wasteland, and Ngati Paoa and Ngati Whatua had left the area in fear of further Ngapuhi raids – scattering to hide in the ranges to the east of Kaipara and to the west of Auckland, with many seeking refuge to the south in Ngati Paoa and Waikato territory.

There was a similar story in north Taranaki (around New Plymouth), where the emigration of Te Atiawa to escape the ravages of the Waikato tribes had also left that land empty.

Such fighting and destruction was a feature of Maori society before colonisation which, with its central authority, brought peace among the tribes. Cannibalism was usual, with survivors kept as slaves. War was a delight, a challenging sport and a way to gain renown and position.

That violence was supported by, and stimulated by, the old culture, the *tikanga*. Loyalty was to the tribe, and members of other tribes

---

[26] Stone 2001, pages 79-107
[27] Robinson 2020, pages 16, 23, 32, 37, 65

were not considered as fellow human beings. The demands of *utu*, revenge for past perceived wrongs, kept disputes alive, often expanding far beyond the initial incident. There was no other way of conflict resolution than armed might. The Maori world was in disarray; this was a 'failed state', with a broken society.

In *tikanga*, there were considerable class and caste differences, between chiefs, commoners and slaves, between men and women.[28] Later settlers were to notice the considerable difference between the sexes. "The men for the most part are fine athletic fellows, but I regret to say I cannot bestow any praise on the appearances of the women, who were without exception the most degraded, hideous, dirty set of human beings I have ever set my eyes upon." [29]

"The females are not in general so handsome as the men ... they are burdened with all the heavy work; they have to cultivate the fields, to carry from their distant plantations wood and provisions, and to bear heavy loads during their travelling excursions." [30]

"The women generally do the whole of the planting and the gathering in of the crops. The first thing in the morning, the New Zealand female may be seen fetching a back-load of fire-wood to prepare the morning's meal – after which, the plantation grounds engrosses her attention until mid-day, when she proceeds to the sea-beach to gather cockles, and at night, she brings in another back-load of wood to cook the supper; if she has a child that is too young to walk, the father takes care of it, unless he is going fishing or to war – in either case, of course, the mother has a double duty to attend to. It is no uncommon thing to observe her carrying upwards of a hundred weight on her back, up a steep hill, for the men will not degrade themselves by carrying provisions, particularly on their backs. ... They [the women]

---

[28] Robinson 2012, pages 23-41
[29] From the Journal of surveyor R H Aubrey, quoted in Wells 1878, page 56. On page 61 Wells quotes similar observations by Cutfield to the Director of the Plymouth Company. Both were writing in 1841.
[30] Dieffenbach 1843, page 11

have the appearance of being aged, when about twenty-five to thirty – and after about thirty-five they become truly ugly …" [31]

The situation of women became much worse when the fighting intensified. They were raped, killed and eaten, enslaved, or 'taken to wife' (as concubines). Some spoke of their despair.

"On taxing some females with having committed infanticide, they laughed heartily at the serious manner in which I put the question. They told me the poor infants did not know or care much about it. One young woman, who had recently destroyed a female infant, said that she wished her mother had done the same to her, when she was young; 'For why should my infant live?' she added; 'to dig the ground! to be a slave to the wives of her husband! to be beaten by them, and trodden under foot! No! can a woman here protect herself, as among the white people'?" [32]

We must never forget the reality of the horrors of the existence of those people living in New Zealand when there was no law or security, and *tikanga* was the ruling culture.

---

[31] *Sydney Herald*, 3 July 1837. "Sketches of New Zealand"
[32] Polack 1838; Robinson 2019, page 88

Cultural transformation, the new Maori society

The decades of the 1830s and beyond witnessed a complete transformation in Maori society, in beliefs and way of life.[33] The cultural revolution was complete, from the old superstitions of *tikanga* and *matauranga Maori* to Christianity, from tribalism to becoming part of a united nation, from insecurity, warfare, slavery and cannibalism to peace, from old lore to new law with a new way of conflict resolution, from class and caste privileges (with exploitation of commoners and slaves) towards equality.

The destruction of the first forty years of the nineteenth century, when *tikanga* ruled, was evident and some Maori chiefs began to seek a better way. At first, they were blocked by adherence to their traditional beliefs.

One of the most penetrating insights into Maori perspectives on war, and the initial failure of missionary efforts to bring peace, is provided by the record of an 1825 conference with seven leading Ngapuhi chiefs convened by the missionaries in Kerikeri.[34]

Hongi Hika described how the imperatives of *tikanga* prevented them from giving up war as a way of life. When the missionaries spoke of the many benefits of European civilisation, Hongi replied of the hold of the old way: "They must have their bad hearts thrown away before they can see the good of these things." Pakira recognised how deeply

---

[33] Robinson 2012 "A new and peaceful culture", pages 87-92; Robinson 2015; Robinson 2016 "Maori cultural revolution and calls for help,1830s", pages 20-24; Robinson 2019 "Changes of Maori culture, from traditional *tikanga*", pages 98-114
[34] Cloher 2003, pages 44-51and 190. His source is Davis 1825. This discussion is reported in full in Robinson 2015, pages 35-43, and summarised in Robinson 2019, pages 95-96

imbued Maori were with the propensity to fight: "Our war and fighting were sown into our hearts by our parents as your learning was sown into your hearts by your parents." Although Hongi appreciated the missionaries' stance and agreed that war is a "bad thing indeed", he could not shift away from his own position, saying: "My heart is as hard as a piece of wood. I cannot stop".

But gradually the horrors of the warfare, which were widespread, across the whole country, and the teachings of the missionaries, telling of a different religion and way of life, began to lead to a greater desire for change. There was a great move to Christianity and 'a decade of change' between 1830 and 1840.[35] "During this decade the changes in Maori life and society had become irreversible. They had not, of course, affected all tribes equally, but they had spread like a contagion far beyond the areas of direct European contact. The pattern of society and the rules regulating it had by 1840 been fundamentally changed. ... the 1830s marked the watershed. From then on, there could be no turning back."[36]

Many Maori had been seeking a way to escape the terrible consequences of the requirement of their culture for never-ending revenge, *utu*, and asked for the intervention of missionaries and then the colonial regime, who provided an alternative approach to conflict resolution and a cover for their moves away from the old *tikanga*.[37]

"Around 1831 Fenton noted the desolation produced by war in the Thames district, about Tamaki and extending far to the north, including deserted villages along the coast by the Bay of Islands. He wrote 'Christianity has begun to make some progress, and wearied and worn out by war, the people appear to have hastily and gladly embraced the new religion which ... secured to them ... a tolerable

---

[35] Robinson pages 88-89; Wilson 1985, Chapters 7 and 9
[36] Wilson 1985, page 167
[37] Robinson 2019, pages 103-112

certainty of keeping their bodies in peace in this world until the time came for them to die naturally'."[38]

That year, 1831, thirteen Ngapuhi chiefs and the Church Missionary Society missionaries – principally William Yate – gathered at Kororipo Pa to compose a letter to the British government, addressed to King William IV, with a desire for settled law and order and a call for help to Britain ("to become our friend and the guardian of these islands").[39] That plea was answered by the appointment in 1833 of James Busby as Consular Agent, the inaugural British Resident.

Busby explained that British action could only follow a treaty with a sovereign power, a central authority that did not exist in a warring tribal society. Following discussions with northern chiefs, he drafted a letter proposing such a central authority, which was presented to a meeting of thirty-four northern Maori chiefs at his residence at Waitangi on 28 October, 1835.[40]

The letter included an entreaty to the King of England "that he will continue to be the parent of their infant State, and that he will become its Protector from all attempts upon its independence." This proposed new state would be reliant on British help.

The intention was to form a "Confederation of the United Tribes", which did not exist at the time. A call went out to the Southern tribes to join that confederation, but that worthy effort failed. Later, another 18 chiefs signed; the only two outside the north were Te Wherowhero (who, in 1835, had become a peacemaker in Mangere, see chapter 'Peace agreements, Auckland') and Te Hapuku of Hawke's Bay, during a visit to the Bay of Islands in September 1838. As missionary William Yate noted, "There is no national bond of union amongst

---

[38] Sherrin 1890, page 379
[39] Sherrin 1890, page 381; Walker 1990, page 87; Robinson 2015, pages 56-59
[40] Robinson 2012, pages 93-100; Robinson 2015, pages 60-66

them; each one is jealous of the authority and power of his neighbour."[41]

By 1838-39 it had become clear that the only way to protect Maori and settlers alike was for New Zealand to become a colony. The British finally decided to act, to take the only possible practical step – to reach some agreement with Maori through a treaty and to form a colonial administration.

The Treaty of Waitangi was what the northern chiefs wanted, an answer to their calls for help.

---

[41] Yate 1835, page 114

The real Treaty of Waitangi

The Treaty of Waitangi was a significant part of the Maori cultural transformation, following two previous Maori requests for British involvement in New Zealand.

The northern chiefs had realised that the only way forward would be to hand sovereignty to the British and become a colony with a central government and system of laws that would bring peace with an end to the tribal separation and warfare. Thus, when the British decided to ask for their agreement the chiefs were ready to act.

This was to be a new form of colonisation, 'Humanitarian Colonisation'. The British authorities recognised a common humanity and understood the challenges of dealing with very different cultures – as noted in a "Report upon the best Means of Promoting the Civilization of the Aboriginal Inhabitants of Australia" that Captain George Grey (later twice Governor, and then Premier, of New Zealand) had prepared, based on his experiences in Australia, and this was forwarded by the Secretary of State in 1840 to Lieutenant-Governor Hobson.[42] "They are as apt and intelligent as any other race of men I am acquainted with; they are subject to the same affections, appetites, and passions as other men."[43]

When he came to New Zealand to propose and agree to a treaty, Hobson was provided with many instructions of what was intended. The good intentions are set down in a despatch from Lord John Russell to Lieutenant-Governor Hobson (9 December, 1840). "It is, however, impossible to cast the eye over the map of the globe, and to discover so much as a single spot where civilised men brought into contact with tribes differing from themselves widely in physical structure, and greatly inferior to themselves in military prowess and

---

[42] Grey 1840; Robinson 2015, pages 75-76
[43] Grey 1840; Robinson 2015, pages 75-76; Robinson 2016, page 28

social arts, have abstained from oppressions and other evil practices. In many, the process of extermination has proceeded with appalling rapidity. ... Be the causes, however, of this so frequent calamity what they may, it is our duty to leave no rational experiment for the protection of it unattempted. ... The aborigines of New Zealand will, I am convinced, be the objects of your constant solicitude, as certainly there is no subject connected with New Zealand which the Queen, and every class of Her Majesty's subjects in this kingdom, regard with more settled and earnest anxiety."[44]

The final text of the Treaty was prepared in the days following the arrival of Hobson in New Zealand. After consideration of a number of suggestions and drafts set down over several days of discussions in February, 1840, a final copy was decided upon, and written down by James Busby, on February 4. This was translated into Maori, to be presented to the chiefs on February 5.

This was a straightforward, clear document. Here it is, the original copy, now known as the Littlewood Treaty.[45]

"Article first

The chiefs of the Confederation of the United Tribes and the other chiefs who have not joined the confederation cede to the Queen of England for ever the entire Sovreignty [sic] of their country.

Article Second

The Queen of England confirms and guarantees to the chiefs and tribes and to all the people of New Zealand the possession of their lands, dwellings and all their property. But the chiefs of the Confederation and the other chiefs grant to the Queen the exclusive right of purchasing such land as the proprietors thereof may be

---

[44] BPP 1840, pages 27-28; Robinson 2016, page 31
[45] Doutré 2005

disposed to sell at such prices as shall be agreed upon between them and the person appointed by the Queen to purchase from them.

Article Third

In return for the cession of the Sovreignty to the Queen, the People of New Zealand shall be protected by the Queen of England, and the rights and privileges of British subjects will be granted to them."

Here is:

1. the transformation of sovereignty, agreed to by the Maori leaders of the day, the chiefs, and recognised subsequently by chiefs on many occasions, as at the 1860 Kohimarama meeting[46],
2. the promise that all of New Zealand that had not been properly sold belonged to Maori (a promise that was kept as most sales before 1840 were not accepted by the Commissioner, William Spain), and that land properly purchased belonged to the buyers (note the significant inclusion of 'all the people of New Zealand'),
3. provision to all people living in New Zealand of the full rights and duties of British citizenship.

That last Article most significantly includes all non-Maori living here; New Zealanders were recognised as equal from the very first – this was the basic principle of the new nation, that we are one people. **Any move from that principle is the breaking of the treaty.**

The final copy in English (quoted above), written by James Busby, and dated February 4, was mislaid until it was discovered in 1989, and is known as the 'Littlewood Treaty'. It is the same as a copy in English sent by James Reddy Clendon to the USA immediately

---

[46] Robinson 2022

following the first signing, and other early translations. There is one treaty; both Maori and English copies are the same.

Unfortunately, in the few days after the signing of the treaty, Clendon left the original English text with his lawyer, Littlewood, and Hobson's secretary, James Freeman, produced a new version, making use of the earlier draft notes, which he sent to Australia on February 8. This has since sat in the archives and has become known as the 'English Treaty'.

Incredibly, this cobbled together and inaccurate version of the Treaty of Waitangi has been accepted from then to the present day, and official accounts are that there are two very different Treaties of Waitangi (as noted in a later chapter, 'Rewriting the Treaty of Waitangi').

After the ritual challenges of the afternoon of February 5, 1840, the chiefs felt no need for any further discussion. They gathered the following morning to sign and return, satisfied, home. Hobson, who had expected a longer debate, had to be woken up and brought ashore for the ceremony. The speed of the proceedings showed clearly that the matter had been well thought through in advance; it satisfied the Maori desires. **The call for the British to come and the enthusiastic signing of the treaty were largely Maori initiatives, and significant features of the Maori cultural transformation.**

Peace agreements, Auckland, around 1840

The Auckland area is rich in natural resources, with fertile soil and plentiful seafood from both the Waitemata and Manukau Harbours. But (as noted previously), by 1833 the Tamaki isthmus seemed a man-made desert and Henry Williams wrote that the land was overgrown and no sign of an inhabitant could be seen in any direction[47]; in 1835, "the once-populous lands bordering the Waitemata remained deserted ... there were no people living in this land at that time."[48]

By the 1830s many chiefs in the north and centre of the North Island were becoming weary of the ravages of war (while savage fighting was to continue through that decade to the south). The formerly aggressive northern Ngapuhi of Hongi Hika (who had died in 1828), had listened to the messages of missionaries and wanted to move away from their previous warlike ways.

The former people of Auckland were scattered; they had suffered from the consequences of savage inter-tribal warfare and wished for peace, to return to their fertile lands and to live with security, free from those many previous frequent attacks.

Perhaps the greatest warrior chief of the time, Te Wherowhero of Waikato (later the first, pacifist, Maori king), had also become a peace-maker. When some Ngati Whatua moved to the Manukau from the Waikato Heads in 1835, he escorted them and provided protection. Te Wherowhero moved from Ngaruawahia to a strategic *pa* on the south side of the Manukau and Ngati Whatua took up residence nearby. However, in spite of the presence of Te Wherowhero, those who returned did not at first feel secure.[49]

---

[47] Stone 2001, pages 126-9
[48] Stone 2001, page 152
[49] Stone 2001, page 151-153

Missionaries made efforts to aid the progressive resettlement. In 1835, Henry Williams and Rev. Robert Maunsell went by ship with a group of Ngai Tahu led by Rewa, who had been a fearsome warrior but was now a Christian and a peacemaker, to make peace with Ngati Paoa at Thames. The basis of reconciliation was an agreement over the disputed borderland south of Otahuhu. This was to be transferred to the Anglican missionaries, who would then hold it in trust as a buffer zone between the two tribes. The 1836 conciliation meeting was at Otahuhu, in the presence of Te Wherowhero, who agreed to the plan of the missionaries. It was decided that the putative purchaser of the land would be William Fairburn, and this extensive area became known as the 'Fairburn purchase".

The missionary plan was a way of helping the negotiating chiefs to move away from the dictates of *tikanga*: "By making this particular block of land the pretext for reconciliation, the two powerful but war-weary chiefs could make concessions on territory of less than vital interest to themselves, and thereby give way without loss of *mana*."[50]

By 1837, some Ngati Whatua wanted to move further into their former territory, near their gardens in the fertile volcanic soils of Mangere, which would move them from the protective shield of Te Wherowhero. The solution was the gift from Ngati Whatua of some land near Onehunga and not far from Three Kings, so that the visits of Te Wherowhero would establish a protective presence.

The Anglican missionaries in the Bay of Islands carried out education work, with a system of combined annual examinations, which were well attended, by families as well as students. They found that these examination *hui* offered an occasion for meeting and the burying of differences between members of estranged tribes who attended, and decided to repeat the procedure in Tamaki, on the neutral land of the Fairburn purchase.

---

[50] Stone 2001, page 161-168

The annual examination of students on the neutral ground at Otahuhu in 1837, organised by the three missionaries, provided a place for a series of informal meetings between elders of the tribes. The missionaries found the chiefs were ready to talk peace and, "in a new spirit of amity the tribes went their separate ways, Te Taou to Mangere, Ngati Te Ata to Awhitu, Ngati Tamaoho to the inner Manakau, and Ngati Paoa to Waiheke, Maraetai and points south."[51]

When, in 1840, the British sent Hobson to propose a treaty with British sovereignty, which would bring peace across the country, there remained a fear in Auckland of neighbours to the north and others to the south (as described by Percy Smith). "According to Smith, such was the 'state of unrest' in the region at the time that shortly after the news of Hobson's arrival at the Bay of Islands reached the Waitemata, a meeting was called of the remnants of the tribes at Okahu, near the future City of Auckland, to determine on what course they should pursue to ensure their safety. This conference was widely attended. Its convenor, Te Whatarangi, was able to draw in (said one account) all the great chiefs of the Tamaki, Waitemata, Kaipara, and other surrounding districts.

The prolonged discussion at this gathering as to how the tribes could best secure peace and order and a cessation of war and strife was inconclusive. It was thought that enduring peace would only come to the Waitemata if the newly arrived governor were invited to establish his power there. The suggestion was acted on. An embassy of chiefs headed by Te Reweti Tamaki (Te Kawau's nephew) – described by Terry as 'very acute and intelligent, particularly as to the interests of his tribe, in all his transactions with Europeans' – travelled north to persuade Hobson to shift his seat of government to Tamaki."[52]

---

[51] Stone 2001, page 176-179
[52] Stone 2001, pages 185-6

Hobson soon looked around for the site of a possible capital, and made the choice of Auckland. Further peacemaking and reconciliation between Ngati Whatua and Ngati Paoa took place in 1841 and 1842, with a name given to the occasion "the blotting out of the transgressions of the people".[53] It was not until Tamaki became the site of the capital, with the concomitant prospect of the governor's peace and of enriching trade, that Ngati Whatua felt they could safely resettle many of their people back at Orakei.

There were other similar negotiations. In 1844, Te Wherowhero and the Waikato people gave a great *hakari* or feast at Remuera in Auckland in return for a feast provided by Hauraki chiefs the preceding year. The principal political objective was to settle the dispute over Motiti Island off the Tauranga coast. The following year: "Peace was concluded after years of war between the allied peoples of Maketu, Rotorua and Taupo on one side and the Tauranga and Waikato Maoris on the other."[54]

There is much to learn here for the New Zealand of the early twenty-first century.

Auckland society had been destroyed by Maori wars, by the Maori way of life. Peace came only with many genuine efforts, over around ten years of meetings, negotiations and agreements – putting it all together again took many efforts of chiefs, of missionaries, and of the British colonial government, all working together in a new spirit, guided by the introduced ideals of Christianity. Not by separation.

Now, in 2022, New Zealand is splitting apart, with peoples branded by race and separated by race. It is time to remember the successes of past healing, to return to basic principles of a common humanity and again to heal the wounds opening up across our society. That cannot happen in the absence of dialogue, as today, with Maori keeping separate and developing

---

[53] Stone 2001, page 190
[54] Fraser 1986, pages 27 and 28; Robinson 2015, pages 92-94

a national apartheid constitution at so many *hui* away from other fellow New Zealanders, aided by distorted historical accounts and education, and news controlled to prevent any open debate, with the focus on past conflicts rather than on the way that all New Zealanders once chose to come together.

Freeing slaves, Waikato 1842

The great advances of the cultural transformation, accompanied by Christianity and colonisation, included the end of tribal warfare, cannibalism and slavery, together with security of land ownership and freedom. Such a complete social revolution was a complex and lengthy process, not all smooth sailing, as these advances brought further problems. The rights of both Maori and newcomers were to be respected (all being British citizens): previous land sales were tested, and some outrageous claims were rejected, while others, reasonable and fair, were recognised.

Those Maori who had been dispossessed and scattered in the wars were now free to return to their former homelands. In some cases, most notably in north Taranaki, much of that land had been sold fairly by those left behind, and it proved difficult to sort out the mess; the rights of the new owners had to be recognised, along with those of the returning peoples. There had to be some settlement under the new system of law, with decisions on the conflicting desires and rights. These decisions, with the associated uncertainty and clashes with Maori ways (as understood, differently, by different actors in the unfolding drama), would lead to further difficulties, problems that took a time to work through, with the associated disagreements and conflict.

In Maori society, under the *tikanga* that was to be replaced by British law, there had been widespread warfare between the tribes. After battle, many of the defeated would be killed (including women and children) for a great cannibal feast. Survivors were taken as slaves, whose lives were of no value; some were killed for food or a further feast for the *taua*, or later to celebrate an important visit or the death of a chief. Slaves carried out much of the drudgery in that wartime economy. They had no rights and could be killed with impunity, sometimes in anger or by a jealous wife.[55]

Thus, following the defeat of Te Atiawa at Pukerangiora in 1831, it is said at least 200 who had attempted to flee the siege died immediately, with Te Wherowhero killing 150 single-handedly with blows to the head. The scene that followed was terrible, with huge numbers of the dead gutted and spit-roasted over fires. In desperation, women threw their children off the cliff into the Waitara River and jumped in after them, rather than have them captured alive. It is thought that as many as 1,200 Te Atiawa lost their lives.

Many captives were then taken as slaves back to the Waikato. Leaving only a handful of people, the remaining Te Atiawa began the long trek south to Kapiti, and the whole of north Taranaki was left depopulated, apart from a pocket of land around New Plymouth.[56]

"Since the removal of the majority, the small remnant of the original natives of Taranaki had lived a very agitated life, often harassed by the Waikato, and seeking refuge on one of the Rocky Sugarloaf Islands, at times dispersed into the impenetrable forests at the base of Mount Egmont, sometimes making a temporary truce with their oppressors, but always regarded as an enslaved and powerless tribe."[57]

In November, 1939, Colonel Wakefield purchased a considerable area of the southern North Island for the New Zealand Company from Te Atiawa at Waikanae (which sale was not later recognised). About the same time, Taranaki was purchased a second time, from a different group of Te Atiawa, at New Plymouth. These were the remnant Maori, left in occupation after slaves had been taken to Waikato and a group of warriors and their families had gone south.

---

[55] Robinson 2012, page 29
[56] Robinson 2016, page 17; Robinson 2020, pages 88-89
[57] Dieffenbeck, reported in Wells 1878, pages 21 and 23; Robinson 2012, pages 145-146

"Many of the true owners were absent, while others had not returned from slavery to the Waikatos in the north."[58] Those remaining appeared to be living a wretched existence.[59]

Those few remnants had been eager to sell land in 1839 and gain the protection of the British settlers.[60] However, the arrival of those settlers in 1841 attracted the Waikato who felt that the land was theirs, by conquest. A well-armed party came and "caused some distress". They were given presents and "induced to return in peace to Waikato", and Te Wherowhero agreed to part with his claim to the land.[61]

Then in 1842, following vigorous discussions among the Waikato tribes of whether to keep or release their slaves, the newly freed slaves returned from the Waikato: "a considerable number of natives have lately been liberated by the Waikatos, who, some years ago, overran the Taranaki district, and carried off a large portion of its inhabitants as slaves."[62]

"The Rev. Samuel Ironside, Wesleyan Missionary, thus speaks of the return of the Ngatiawa from captivity in Waikato: Waikato hearing of the sale of lands at Taranaki by those whom they deemed their slaves, were very angry, and resolved to come down in force, and utterly destroy the remnant there. But there were many sincere Christians in Waikato, chiefly under the care of Rev. John Whitely, at Kawhia, and the Rev. James Wallace at Whaingaroa. These Christian natives opposed the design of their heathen relatives, and farther, resolved to give freedom to their Taranaki slaves, and escort them back to their native place. At the annual meeting of the Wesleyan ministers stationed in and near Waikato, in May 1842, I

---

[58] Houston 1965
[59] Robinson 2012, pages 145-146
[60] Robinson 2016, pages 34-40
[61] Wells 1878, page 77 (the letter quoted is dated December, 1841: Robinson page 146.
[62] Wells 1878, page 85

was directed to go with these Christian natives on their errand of mercy. I went on this journey attended by some hundreds of Waikato natives, Christian and heathen. At Mokau we left all signs of population behind us, and for sixty miles travelled through a silent country. On nearing New Plymouth the few inhabitants, not over twenty, took alarm, hurried into their canoes and paddled off to their rock, leaving the food cooking in their iron pots on the fire. It was only after considerable persuasion that they ventured to come ashore. We spent two or three days in discussion, and at length, the Waikato natives receiving a large portion of the purchase money for the country, and firing off their guns in memory of their dead there, and in token of their rights, returned home leaving the poor Taranaki people in peace." [63]

However, the freed slaves who had returned from captivity in the Waikato were unhappy with the sale of their lands. "The manumitted natives are now returning to this district, and not having been party to the sale of the land to the Company, now complain that they have neither potato grounds nor *utu* in money or recompense. I cannot discover among the malcontents a single person who, according to the custom of the natives, has or had a right to sell the land. On the contrary, many who did sell the land have distinctly warned me not to enter into any bargain or treaty with these returned slaves." [64]

There were furious arguments and threats of violence, and some disruption to the activities of the colonists in those uncertain times. In 1842 the disputes calmed down when Maori were told of the coming investigation by Commissioner Spain, when appropriate awards could be made. However soon after: "A body of armed natives drove Messrs, Goodall and Brown ... off their section. ... the real chiefs assured me that the rioters had no claim whatsoever to the land, and only intended to terrify me into paying *utu*." But some disruption continued "I have had some trouble with Maoris, not

---

[63] Wells 1878, pages 90 and 91
[64] Wells 1878, page 85

Waikatos, at the Waitara. A number of men, belonging to Kapiti, have appeared among the Waitara people and ... stopped a party of surveying men. ... The natives have continued to cut down the bush and timber on Mr. Cooke's section, and have extended their devastation to Mr. Marshall's."[65]

The ruling by Commissioner Spain in 1844 was that the 1839 sale at New Plymouth was valid; he decided that the few who remained in occupation in 1839 had every right to sell their Taranaki land. The award was for 60,000 acres to the New Zealand Company, upholding their purchase, with 6,000 acres to Maori (the tenths, native reserves) as well as 120 acres currently in cultivation, and 100 acres to the Wesleyan Missionary Society for mission land.

Many Maori, the freed slaves who had returned from captivity in the Waikato, and others who had drifted back to settle on their previous land, as well as Te Atiawa living in Wellington and Kapiti, were disappointed, and angry. Robert Fitzroy, the second Governor of New Zealand, gave in to the threats of forceful action, and reversed Spain's decision. This gave the impression that intimidation could prevail over the law, and the concept of a clear law, administered by the central authority, was shattered.[66]

Although living in Waikanae, and having signed a sale of Taranaki land back in 1839, the Te Atiawa chief Wiremu Kingi was determined to have Waitara. He and his warriors returned there in 1848, breaking an agreement with Governor Grey (the third Governor) to keep to the north side of the Waitara River.[67]

There was then no effective regional authority to keep the peace in Taranaki, either by local Maori or by the national government. There had long been quarrels among Te Atiawa, which were further stimulated by their dispersal and then return to a place where land

---

[65] Wicksteed to Colonel Wakefield. Wells 1878, pages 85, 97 and 102
[66] Robinson 2016, pages 52-67
[67] Robinson 2016, pages 89-93

ownership was disputed. There was an increase in tribal feuds, with fighting throughout the following years.[68]

In 1859, Governor Gore Browne went to Taranaki, where he spoke on two subjects, the Maori feuds and land purchase, which he said he wanted to be considered separately, as having no sort of reference to each other. He then recognised the failure of Government to maintain the law on several previous occasions, and a determination to do so from then on.

This provided an opportunity for those who wished to sell land. "Almost immediately after McLean finished reading the Governor's speech, one chief, Teira, stood up and, saying that 'he had heard with satisfaction the declaration of the Governor referring to individual claims, and the assurance of protection that would be afforded', he offered to sell land (600 acres) on the Waitara. This was opposed by others in this divided, warring community but the challenge had to be met and the Governor agreed to accept providing that Teira could prove his title."[69] This was to lead to rebellion by a group led by Kingi, who refused to accept the decision of the appointed commissioner.[70]

Here was an unfortunate consequence of the steady process of British humanitarian colonisation. In the years immediately following the signing of the Treaty most Maori were ready to accept the newly introduced law, which would be explained to them. However, clarity was destroyed by Fitzroy. Meanwhile, the new colonial government lacked the desire and the force to assert the law and to insist on changes, such as the end of slavery and acceptance of a clear law on land ownership; rather they preferred to leave Maori to organise their own affairs.

---

[68] Robinson 2012, pages 147-150; Robinson 2016, pages 94-101
[69] Robinson 2016, pages 139-145
[70] Robinson 2016, pages 152-153

This time of uncertainty, of seeking for a reasoned judgement, was made more difficult by the conflicting precepts (guidelines) of *tikanga*, a tribal way of thinking that had never developed to face such a challenge and which included a variety of ways to claim ownership.

What was to be recognised ownership as tribal lore was replaced by British law? The system was new. Before colonisation an area under the control of a tribe would be defined by the reality of conquest or defeat, as well as claims based on previous settlement. One question that arose concerned which period of occupation should be recognised, or given prior importance, when many places that had been previously settled for centuries had changed hands in the few decades preceding the Treaty of Waitangi.

Then, too, some rights were held in common by the tribe while individual plots of land would be used by a family group, a second form of ownership. Which had priority, now that the rule of chiefs was diminished by the new rights of all as British citizens? The absolute power of chiefs had gone while the tribal way of life continued. The resulting conflict between tribal and individual rights was to prove grounds for conflict.

This is seen most dramatically in the words of Kingi in a letter to the Governor: "I will not agree to our bedroom being sold (I mean Waitara here), for this bed belongs to the whole of us".[71] Yet in his response when payment was made to Teira and others for land at Waitara. Kingi was asked: "Does the land belong to Teira and his party?" His answer was: "Yes, the land is theirs, but I will not let them sell it."

At the core of Kingi's rebellion was his demand to be the arbiter, to sweep aside the new law and make rulings that would favour his

---

[71] AJHR 1860 E-2, no. 82, page 229, "Wiremu Kingi to the Governor", Waitara, 25th April, 1859

interests against those of others in the tribe. Tribal rule could not co-exist with a national authority.

That dispute was within Maori society; it was no wrong of colonisation, which was faced with how best to introduce a new legal system. Sadly, the current focus on conflict has led to a loss of memory, forgetting one of the many great benefits of colonisation – freedom for slaves.

One very real failure was the long delay experienced by the enslaved Moriori of the Chatham Islands before they gained their freedom. They had been attacked by Ngati Mutunga (who had moved on from Kapiti and Wellington) in 1835, when around 300 Moriori were killed (early accounts did not include the considerable number of children killed, whose names had been forgotten). Those remaining were taken as slaves. Women were taken as concubines and men were kept in servile bondage, and often traded as payment for seeds or pork. Many died subsequently of despair. One list suggests that only 101 Moriori were still alive in 1862, and Moriori remained enslaved until 1863.[72] There is no supposed wrong of colonisation that comes anywhere near matching the horror of the Moriori experience, which had been carried out by Maori under the guidance of their traditional culture. *Tikanga* brought slavery; colonisation brought freedom.

February 6, 1840, with the acceptance and signing of the Treaty of Waitangi, was the date of the emancipation of slaves in New Zealand, with equality of all living here: "the People of New Zealand shall be protected by the Queen of England, and the rights and privileges of British subjects will be granted to them." We must never forget this glorious milestone in the development of our nation.

---

[72] King 2000, pages 58-67; Robinson 2020, pages 94-95

Great meeting of chiefs, Kohimarama 1860

In the decades after the signing of the Treaty, there was frequent co-operation between chiefs and the central colonial government; all were working together towards a common goal, of a peaceful and successful nation.

As already explained, the disturbances among Te Atiawa following the return to Taranaki of slaves from the Waikato, and then others who had previously migrated to Kapiti, brought disputes over land sales. In 1860 Kingi had refused to accept the decision of the law, would not allow the sale of some land at Waitara, and led a rebellion that soon led to armed conflict. At that same time, a separatist king movement, which hoped to set up a separate kingdom, had been formed in the Waikato, largely a coalition of tribes formed during the musket wars several decades before (those led by Waharoa). There were fears that the country would descend again into the chaos of war between conflicting tribal groups.

Some hundreds of chiefs from across the country then joined a great meeting at Kohimarama, now Mission Bay, Auckland, to express their concerns and common goals. They made clear the desires of most Maori for peace, in opposition to those malcontents who were raising the flag of rebellion and threatening the existence and development of the unified nation.[73]

They affirmed their loyalty to the Crown, with forthright resolution. "That this Conference takes cognizance of the fact that the several Chiefs, members thereof, are pledged to each other to do nothing inconsistent with their declared recognition of the Queen's sovereignty, and of the union of the two races; also to discountenance

---

[73] Robinson 2022

all proceedings tending to a breach of the covenant here solemnly entered into by them."

As one speaker, Tukihaumene, said: "Let the Queen's Sovereignty spread and extend to every place. From the Reinga (in the north) to where the sun rises, and on to Port Nicholson. The acknowledgment of the Queen has been agreed to by us all."

There was similar recognition of the Treaty of Waitangi by many speakers. Thus, Hemi Metene Te Awaitaia: "That was the union of races at Waitangi. I was there at the time, and I listened to the love of the Queen. I then heard about the advantages of the treaty." And Tamihana Te Rauparaha: "The Treaty of Waitangi also is good. The object of these is to unite the Pakeha and the Maori."

While recognising the Crown and the undoubted benefits of colonisation, the chiefs believed that the biggest gift brought by British, which they celebrated frequently and enthusiastically, was Christianity. This new religion and its associated worldview had brought about the most important changes in their great cultural transformation. Some typical viewpoints were:

"In my opinion the greatest blessings are, Christianity and the Laws." (Hemi Metene Te Awaitaia)

"In former times all men were as orphans, (friendless,) and every tribe sought for some means by which they might return and live. When the Gospel was made known to us, we sought it as the means of saving men's lives. We were told that it was a good thing and would save the soul. We accepted it. We submitted to the law of God." (Hone Waiti)

"The first thing which absorbed my attention was Christianity. It was brought here by the Missionaries. Subsequently a Governor came, and good things began to flourish in New Zealand." (Hamiora Tu)

"It was the law of Christianity that put an end to our cannibal practices." (Tamihana Te Raupahara)

There was a general wish for greater integration, and a more active role for Maori in applying the law.

All were strongly opposed to the actions of Kingi in Taranaki and the king movement in the Waikato, with a rejection of rebellion, concern with the future, and a common desire that those disruptive movements would die away. It was hoped that negotiations would bring an end to conflict.

The arrival of Maori voyagers in the 13th century. Standing at the foot of the mast is the white-haired tohunga, making an invocation to the gods. From an oil painting by Oriwa T. Haddon.

A mission station (Tangiteroria)

A whaling ship with lookout men in fore and main cross-trees, and boats hanging from davits ready to lower away at the cry of "thar she blows!" from the sharp-eyed watchers aloft.

A long, slim whale boat from the Old Whaling Days.

Sir George Grey and three chiefs whom he befriended

Tamati Waka Nene

Te Whero Whero

Rewi Maniapoto

Peace celebrations at Waitara, Taranaki, 1878.

The shipment of frozen meat from New Zealand to Britain began in 1882 when the "Dunedin," shown here, loaded the first cargo at Port Chalmers.

Peace celebration at Waitara, 1878

Despite the considerable efforts of the British, and many New Zealanders (of all ethnicities), the conflict spread and there was further war.[74]

When the fighting in the Waikato against the king movement was over, Auckland and the lower (north) Waikato were safe, with the rebels driven into an area south of the Punui River (just south of Te Awamutu). The government and the Governor (Grey) then made many attempts to bring people together again, and to reach an accommodation with their former foes. A remarkable offer to the defeated rebels in 1878, of the return of most of the confiscated land and even an annual payment of £500, seemed sure of success.[75]

Grey had met twice with the kingites at Te Kopua, in January 1878.[76] He went with the Native Minister, Sheehan, to a third meeting that year at Hikurangi, in May.[77] After preliminary discussions, Tawhiao (the second Maori 'king', the son of Te Wherowhero, who had died in 1860) set down his conditions for the return of much of the Waikato and the division of the nation near Mercer: "Let the Europeans living on this Island go back to the opposite side of that river. Let them have the management of the other side, and let me and the chiefs of the Natives manage this side."

The full satisfaction of that proposal was never possible. However, Grey's response was for a generous settlement leaving much local power with Tawhiao and his fellow chiefs.

---

[74] Robinson 2016
[75] Robinson 2016, pages 336-338
[76] McCan 2001, pages 97-101
[77] AJHR 1878 G-3 *Waikato and Waitara native meetings.* (Reports of meetings between the Hon. the Premier, and the Hon. the Native Minister, and natives.)

"From the answers given by me before about the giving back of Waikato you must know perfectly well that it is impossible for me to do so; but I will tell you what I can do for you.... You are standing in your position with authority, and the Government will add that you are to manage the affairs in your own district, and the Government will assist you with the chiefs of your own districts, so that matters may be conducted in order that peace and good will between the two races of the Island may exist. ... The Government will give you an allowance and the chiefs who are to be your assistants in conducting the affairs within your district. The Government will give you, Tawhiao, £500 a year. The money for distribution within the district will be paid in a lump sum to you, Tawhiao. It is for you to distribute it as you like to the chiefs within your district. The Government will give you 500 acres of land near Ngaruawahia, so as to be close to the grave of your father, Potatau. The Government will erect a house for you at Kawhia, so that you can hold the meetings of your council in it. **The portions of land not disposed of by the Government to Europeans on the western sides of the Waikato and Waipa will be returned to Tawhiao.** ... With regard to the roads, my desire is that all the roads should be managed between Tawhiao and the Government, and that no one else shall interfere – that no one shall attempt to make a road until that matter has been settled by Tawhiao and the Government."[78]

The offer was greeted with acclaim. The expectation amongst most Maori was that the offer would be accepted, and all conflict would be ended. Shortly after, Grey went to see Rewi Maniapoto – formerly the most aggressive and warlike of the kingite chiefs, who had acted many times to stir up and extend conflict – as when he went in 1860 to Taranaki to join the fighting of Kingi at Waitara (against the wishes of the then Maori 'king', the peaceful Te Wherowhero), and when he drove out the British Civil Commissioner, John Gorst, who had been carrying out a useful work, schooling Maori boys and

---

[78] AJHR 1878 G-3, pages 37-38

exercising his magisterial office, from Te Awamutu in 1863 – which had been much appreciated by local Maori.

Rewi was a man of action. He was also a realist; the war was over, his side had lost, and it was time to make peace and move forward together. He immediately announced his intention to move to the next phase of peace-making.

"He starts to-morrow morning early to travel through the lands occupied by his tribe down to Mokau, to proclaim the terms of settlement and procure their concurrence. From Mokau he will proceed to Waitara, and meet William King, the leader of the rebel Natives in the Taranaki war. **At that place he will be met by a number of chiefs from other parts of the Island, and the hatchet will be buried on the spot where it was first used.** He stated that the meeting at Waitara would be at the end of June, and strongly pressed that, if Parliament was not assembled at that time, Sir George Grey and the Native Minister would, if possible, be present at the meeting. Nothing could exceed the kindness and fairness of Rewi throughout the whole talk, and it was evident that a load had been taken off his mind."[79] Rewi Maniapoto had once stood apart as a warmonger; now he became prominent as a peacemaker. The 'king' played no part.

Rewi kept his promise, and the Waitara meeting commenced on June 23, just six weeks later.[80] Many Maori were delighted and came to see their dreams come true; this was what they had waited for and many came with the official party led by the Premier and the Native Minister, including chiefs from "Kapiti, Otaki, Waikanao [sic] and other places". It was arranged that further Native visitors from the Southern districts should come out by train from New Plymouth the following day.[81]

---

[79] AJHR 1878 G-3, page 41; Robinson 2016, pages 338-339
[80] Robinson 2016, pages 340-347
[81] AJHR 1878 G-3, pages 41-42 and 46

There were meetings and conciliation among former foes. Early founders of the king movement, Wi Tako and Matene Te Whiwhi, who had left when support was given to rebels at Waitara, were there. Another early kingmaker, Tamihana Te Rauparaha, had died in 1876. Wiremu Tamihana, who had remained with the movement and made a separate peace in 1865, had died in 1866. Karaitiana, who had always opposed the king movement, was there – Rewi made a point of welcoming these chiefs who had opposed many of his actions. Te Whiti provided about thirty cart-loads of food from Taranaki and voiced his pleasure at being there.

Sir George Grey spoke of the end of conflict and the co-operation among former foes. "Rewi, you asked me to meet you at Waitara that we might discuss certain things together; that we might talk them over together on the very place where the war began. Here I am, in compliance with your invitation, to talk these matters over with you. Since the war began everything has changed. Now, what we have to consider is the future. At the present time the question is not whether you are to be governed by other persons or not, but whether you are to govern yourselves. Now we all stand on an equal footing, Europeans and Natives. We all can unite in choosing the people who are to make the laws for us. The Natives themselves sit in the Houses of Parliament, and help to make laws. The Natives themselves are made Ministers for the purpose of carrying the laws out. We now make one nation together. There is nothing to prevent Natives putting a larger number of Natives in the House as members if they please. There is nothing to prevent Rewi himself, or any other leading chief, entering the Upper House, and helping to carry the laws out. At the present moment the title to their lands is decided by Courts, and not by fighting. We are soon going to try to get an alteration in the law by which the Courts will be much more largely composed of Native Judges who understand Native customs. In fact, every day we are becoming more and more one people."[82]

---

[82] AJHR 1878 G-3, pages 47-48

Rewi responded with similar sentiments. "What you have said is clear. It is right that we should work together for this Island, for us who have caused trouble on the Island. You have come here this day to minister to the ailments of we who brought trouble on the Island, therefore my heart is truly glad; also because Wi Tako, Karaitiana, Matene Te Whiwhi, and other great chiefs are here with you."

Other chiefs celebrated the spirit of friendship, such as Matene te Whiwi to Rewi: You and your European friend, Sir George Grey, invited us here, and by that means we see one another. What I have to say is that I am delighted at what Sir George Grey has uttered this day, and I am also delighted at what he said that you, Rewi, should assist him, and that all the chiefs, present and elsewhere, should help him and support him. I am very much pleased."

Rewi responded with a recognition of past actions. "I brought my misfortunes upon myself. I heard your voice, and though I listened to it, yet my misfortune was of my own creating. I was one of the people who originated the common misfortune, and it is upon this account I asked Sir George Grey to come here. People have talked in all parts of the Island. You, Wi Tako, have done so; but I did not listen to you. Although you gave the word to the people to stop fighting I never heard it. I did not believe your word about stopping the fighting, but allowed the whole country to suffer. I am here at Waitara to meet you and to devise a remedy to save it."

Rewi particularly wanted Karaitiana Takamoana, an early opponent of the king movement who had become a Member of the House of Representatives for Eastern Maori, to be there. Karaitiana was one of the leading chiefs of Hawke's Bay, and, when the King movement first began in the Waikato, he came to Ngaruawahia where he voiced his opposition. "Now you have a King in the island for the Native race. My idea is we cannot have a King, because all the chiefs in New Zealand have signed the treaty of Waitangi, whereby they pledged themselves to come under the Queen, and to obey her laws. We cannot have a King with a few people; we must have a King with a large number of people to govern. We are only a few among so many Europeans. It will only create ill-feeling between the two races if you attempt to set up a King. ...you take your own course, and die in following it. I will take my course, and die in maintaining the laws of the Government. Rewi, you will find my words come true. We shall see each other when my words come to be fulfilled."

Rewi readily recognised the wisdom of that speech. "The words of Karaitiana have come true; we lost all our land and the people."

Their conversation continued in like manner when the two met. Rewi addressed Karaitiana: "You are the man who gave us good counsel in the days that are past, and brought these things before us. We see the evil of them now. We see the evil of rejecting your advice. If we had acted upon your words, we should not have had all the trouble that we passed through. I do not think we should have had any necessity for a meeting at Waitara if your counsel had been adopted. ... I am very glad to see that Sir George Grey, the Native Minister, and yourself are taking these steps to settle all disputes, and to bring a light to the Native race."

Karaitiana then said: "Although you did not listen to me in the early days, my tears are shed in meeting you. They are tears of gladness, and not of sorrow. The Waitara was the first cause of the evil of the Waikato people. The King movement was also another cause of trouble, but that difficulty might have been overcome had the Waitara war not occurred. At the time of this King movement, I heard that Sir George Grey was coming out from Home to be again Governor of New Zealand, and I thought that he could prevent any outbreak of disturbance, because Potatau [Te Wherowhero] was his great friend. Now Potatau is dead and gone. I shall be very glad to see the Waikatos and the Ngatimaniapotos come to friendly terms while Sir George Grey has strength and our new Native Minister is in power."[83]

---

[83] AJHR 1878 G-3, page 44

Late in the day of June 28, the discussions arrived at the substantive issue of the future of Waitara. "Rewi said: I have only one word to explain. I wish Sir George Grey to give me back Waitara. ... When I am clear about this I will be prepared to discuss with you about the establishing of schools, the opening of roads, railways, and telegraphs. When this particular subject is settled then I will talk to you about those matters."

Grey asked for time for reflection and gave his response the following day: "Waitara is now given up to both of us. It belongs to us two. This is the proper spot on which we should loose our hands from one another's heads and cease struggling."

After this was interpreted to the Natives, Rewi gave a short explanation of what had just been said. "It is to allow me to have a voice in the settlement of this matter, so that I may be able with Sir George Grey to unloose our hands from off one another's heads. I agree with what Sir George Grey has said. We have this matter of this land in our hands. I agree because there are now two of us to talk over Waitara. I have nothing further to say to Sir George Grey. He has agreed to my request. Do not let the Europeans and Natives of Waitara be alarmed; they are perfectly safe in their places; let them rest safely in their places. Myself and Sir George Grey will talk the matter over."[84]

One can sense the drama played out that day, and the shared relief that at last the Rubicon was crossed. Here was action, no longer only rhetoric.

This, June 29, 1878, was a day to remember, when the long-serving Governor and the most aggressive kingite rebel came together to share the control over the major bone of contention, Waitara, and thus to signify the end of conflict, the healing of wounds.

---

[84] AJHR 1878 G-3, pages 50-51; from the report of the Correspondent of the *New Zealander*

Rewi's success was widely acknowledged. "In 1879 Rewi Maniapoto was 'received like royalty' in Auckland and provided with a house by the government on their side of the *aukati* (the boundary between Crown and Maori territory). This cleared the way for a deal with Ngati Maniapoto that allowed the government to begin building the main trunk railway across their territory in 1885, guaranteeing European access to the *Rohe Potae*."[85]

The Government offer to the king movement of a generous final settlement (May, 1878) sat on the table waiting for a response from Tawhiao until another great meeting, at Te Kopua, which commenced on Wednesday May 7, 1879. A substantial official party, led by Governor Grey and Native Minister Sheehan, with their officials, was accompanied by chiefs from across the country. They came expecting the completion of the 1878 agreement, and another positive step forward in putting an end to conflict.[86]

That hope was quickly extinguished. They were taken by surprise by the negative and aggressive opening statement of Tawhiao, which indicated a complete change of mind. Tawhiao was out of touch with reality, unable to comprehend that he had been defeated in his war of rebellion fifteen years before.

"Sir George Grey has no right to conduct matters on this Island, but I have the sole right to conduct matters in my land – from the North Cape to the southern end. No one else has any right. He (Sir George Grey) has no right to conduct matters in this Island. That is why I say all things must be returned, and sent away from here [meaning all English customs]."[87]

---

[85] *Maintaining Te Kingitanga*, Ministry for Culture and Heritage, URL: http://www.nzhistory.net.nz/politics/maori-king-movement-1860-94/maintaining-te-kingitanga
[86] Robinson 2016, pages 348-351
[87] AJHR 1879 G-2, *Te Kopua meeting (reports, etc., respecting the proceedings)*

That met with forthright condemnation by chiefs present, who had come expecting to witness a friendly and straightforward agreement between Grey and Tawhiao. Yet here was Tawhiao insisting that he was ruler of them all.

Thus, Hone Mohi Tawhia said: "What was said yesterday by Tawhiao was to this effect: Potatau was the man who owned the land from the extreme South to the utmost North. ... I reply in this way. Governor Hobson arrived amongst the Ngapuhis, the Treaty of Waitangi was made, and the whole of my parents came under that treaty. They agreed to hand over all their lands and their bodies and all their heirs after them to be under the power of the Treaty of Waitangi. From the time of my parents until now, as I stand here, they have all been under the Treaty of Waitangi. Our lands, our bodies, our children – they are all under the Treaty of Waitangi. The Treaty of Waitangi was agreed to by all the tribes of the Island as far as Taiaroa. **Secondly, respecting the chieftainship – it belongs to the whole of the people assembled here.**"

Te Wake followed: "The advice yesterday was that we should unite under the King's word. I will not do so; I will not put myself under him; I will have nothing to do with the King."

A chief of Ngati Tuwharetoa, of Taupo, said: "We reply that this tribe of Tuwharetoa is under the shadow of the law and of the Government. The laws of the Government are in my hand, with all their works – not that I am going to sow them in your district, but I am going to sow them in my own district, Taupo, under my own *mana*."

Te Awaitaia was forthright: "I will never agree to what Tawhiao has said – never, never!"

Maihi te Rangikakehe recalled that Arawa had never joined the king movement, which had never met with universal acceptance, and that many who did so had since left: "The King is supposed to be for the whole Island, and should therefore be supported by the whole of the tribes, but they have left him to be upset in the ocean, while they have swam ashore."

Tawhiao's negative response was a refusal of a declared peace, of coming together and working together as one people. He and the former rebels of his tribe were determined to remain separate from the nation, refusing allegiance to the Crown and the national government. That is the backdrop to many of today's separatists within the continuing king movement, with its powerful organisation and bureaucratic structure.

The many chiefs present were aghast. Grey was devastated. "Three times I have had to come to you at very considerable personal trouble and annoyance. I have had many troubles and many discomforts to go through. I have hurt my health by so doing, and my only object in undergoing these fatigues was to serve you. I wished to do you good."[88]

Grey could only withdraw his offer, which was never again repeated. Because of the repeated refusal of the king to accept the sovereignty of the Crown, Waikato lost more land through confiscations than other districts. Whereas two-thirds or more of confiscated land was returned or purchased from Maori in Taranaki, Tauranga and the Bay of Plenty, only one-quarter was returned in the Waikato.

The early aggressive actions of Rewi were set aside and he became a highly respected member of New Zealand society and a good friend of Grey (as Governor and later as Premier). A monument honouring Rewi was erected at Kihikihi in 1894 (the year of Rewi's death) as a personal tribute from Grey with an inscription describing Rewi as a "custodian of harmony between European and Maori".[89]

---

[88] Robinson and Childs 2018, page 77
[89] op cit, page 75

That monument should be recognised as a symbol of our common humanity, and as a major symbol of the coming together of the peoples of New Zealand. We should remember and celebrate that occasion of goodwill, the great peace-making at Waitara in 1878, that marked the end of the nineteenth century fighting in New Zealand. We need to go forward together and not continue dwelling on differences of the past that so many put behind them in 1878.

Sir Apirana Ngata at the centennial celebration of 1940

Apirana Ngata had led an active and fruitful life, as "student reformer, scholar, author, farmer, churchman, businessman, politician, developer of Maori farming, builder of meeting houses, father of the Maori Battalion, supporter of Maori sport, promoter of the Maori cultural revival, teacher, poet, pioneer of sound recording Maori music, promoter of Maori broadcasting, supporter of education, and fund-raiser extraordinaire."[90]

Throughout his life, Ngata played an active role in improving the lot of Maori, continuing the long process of cultural transformation that was under way in the 1830s.[91]

As a youngster he received guidance from his uncle Rapata Wahawaha, who had fought with Ngati Porou and Government forces against the Hauhau rebels. He then went to Te Aute College, which was developing as one of the best secondary schools in the country, providing a thorough scholastic education to prepare Maori for success and leadership in the new nation.

Ngata did well and went on to gain a BA at Canterbury University College, at the same time as another prominent New Zealander, physicist Ernest Rutherford. He refused the opportunity to carry on a career at a prestigious British university, and continued his studies in law, gaining a MA and an LL.B. at the University of Auckland.

Ngata was active in writing and speaking. For example, in 1892 he won the essay prize at Canterbury College, writing on "The Past and

---

[90] Walker 2001, page 12; Robinson 2015, page 281
[91] Robinson 2015

Future of the Maori"[92] – which has been described as "a condensed discussion of Maori myths, traditions and current theories on Maori origins, tribal culture and responses to Christianity and colonisation".[93] It was more than that; eighteen-year-old Ngata was exploring where he stood and developing the framework for his life's work. Ngata, who had lived in a well-off, middle-class household and a boarding school with a British curriculum, and now was attending university, was trying to relate to life on the *marae*.

When the Te Aute College Students Association (TACSA) was formed in 1897, with the objective, "To aid in the amelioration of the condition of the Maori race physically, intellectually, socially and spiritually", Ngata took an active role. He travelled widely and discussed the needs of Maori with many chiefs (as he had done previously during his Te Aute years).

In a series of talks to TACSA, Ngata spoke on a wide range of topics[94]:

- on questions of employment;

- on the importance of political issues;

- there was much concern with the better use of Maori land and reaching a compromise position on the sale of land to the Government and on the Land Court;

- the *kotahitanga* movement met with both ridicule and sympathy (with opposition to separation, a desire for Maori unity);

- Ngata's concern with sexual morality reflected his Christian education;

---

[92] *Evening Post*, Volume XLIV, Issue 135, 7 December 1892, Page 2; Ngata 1892; Ngata 1893
[93] Walker 2001, page 66
[94] Robinson 2015, pages 196-215

- he was highly critical of gatherings, as "Maori meetings of whatever sort are productive of vice and lax morality" and made scathing comments on some features of Maori life: "The whole of Maori life is rotten; Christianity is lukewarm, if not dead; the Maoris are drunken, idle sots; they love not cleanliness; they do not encourage their children to go to school but on the other hand throw obstacles in the way";

- that criticism included health issues: "they run after *Tohungas* and superstitions; and are utterly ignorant of the rudiments of Hygiene and Medicine";

- he often spoke of the poor care provided by traditional *tohunga*, where "prayers to the big gods and the little gods, the gods of the other regions, and the gods of the land, a bath in the early morning in the running brook in the depth of winter, and good solid food, are sufficient for the patients, though in the most advanced stages of consumption";

- comments on the education of Maori girls were conservative, favouring a traditional role for women; they were not seen as leaders but rather as helpers and nurses with educated women providing suitable partners for educated men, and good mothers.

Ngata made many efforts to find a balance between the old and the new, to preserve that which is valuable in Maori life while rejecting harmful features such as *utu* and the activities of *tohunga*. His aim was to find the optimum balance between further change, with improved health and development, and the preservation of chosen elements of a much-valued Maori culture.

Ngata was able to take effective action on many of those concerns when he became the Member of Parliament for Eastern Maori in 1905. (He was an MP 1905-1943, Minister of Native Affairs 1928-1934, and was knighted in 1927.)

The frequently expressed opposition to *tohunga* was acted upon, and the four Maori MPs were unanimous in putting forward, and voting for, the Tohunga Suppression Act in 1907.

By the end of the nineteenth century the Maori economy was struggling; the problems facing any extension of Maori farming were fundamental – lack of capital, uncertain ownership and lack of familiarity with the organisation of a farm. Ngata had considerable experience with farm development and raising of finance, and he made many efforts to develop new schemes, through to the legislation that underpinned Ngata's efforts, the Native Land Claims Adjustment Act, 1929.[95]

He had noted that, as a student: "I resumed the *Pakeha* scheme of education in 1889 to press on with it until 1897. But it was with the clear vision of acquiring thereby the material and mental equipment wherewith to adapt Maori life to the rapidly changing circumstances and to salvage as much as possible of its worth-while elements."[96] Throughout his life, both in Parliament and after, Ngata continued to focus much of his attention on the revitalisation of the Maori culture that had long been a pleasure to him and one of his major interests.[97] "Some maintain that Sir Apirana's most important contribution to his race was the promotion of a revival of Maori culture through his literary work in collecting and publishing Maori *waiata* (songs, chants, poetry) and his revival of Maori arts and crafts which focused on refurbishing *marae* and the building of carved meeting houses."[98]

Because the remaining king movement refused to co-operate with the New Zealand government, health facilities were poor in the Waikato, with a negative impact on Maori health. Following a visit of one of the elite of the king movement, Te Puea, in 1927 with the *Te Pou o Mangawhiri* concert party to raise funds for the construction of a

---

[95] Robinson 2015, pages 234-245
[96] Ngata 1949, pages xxxix-xxxx
[97] Robinson 2015, pages 265-281
[98] McLauchlan et al 1986, page 42

meetinghouse at Ngaurawahia, Ngata joined with her to develop farms and social services in the Waikato, thus bringing Maori separatists within the national umbrella.[99]

When a celebration was planned for the 1940 centennial of the signing of the Treaty, Ngata was unhappy with the focus on the British, and insisted on a Maori presence. He had a meeting house constructed at Waitangi and spoke there, in a radio broadcast, with the opening words: "The meeting house represents the completion, the embodiment of the desire of the Maori not to be divorced from the Waitangi where Maori and *pakeha* concluded the treaty 100 years ago."[100]

He repeated the recognition of the handing over of sovereignty that had been made clear in the words of Tamati Waka Nene at Waitangi in 1840, of the many chiefs at Kohimarama in 1860, and his own 1922 essay on the Treaty[101], reflecting that a decisive moment had come in 1840 and a decision had been reached; there could be no turning back.

"Clause one of the Treaty handed over the sovereignty of New Zealand to Queen Victoria and her descendants for ever. That is the outstanding fact today. That but for the shield of the sovereignty handed over to her majesty and her descendants I doubt whether there would be a free Maori race in New Zealand today."

The particular benefits of British colonisation were recognised: "I doubt whether any native race has been so well treated by a European people as the Maori."

He then moved to the continuing desire of Maori to preserve their identity. "There still remains the thing called the spirit of the Maori people. We want to remain part but a distinct and individual part of

---

[99] Robinson 2015, pages 242-245
[100] Ngata 1940
[101] Ngata 1922

the future inhabitants of this country. The message of the Maori race to you is: we want to retain our individuality as a race. If that by your standards we fall short, try and look at it from a Maori standpoint – so long as we are happy does it matter very much if we square up with the *pakeha* standards or not. Are they so very good that we should square up to them? Let us achieve health, comfort, happiness. We're on the way to that now thanks to the policies of the government in New Zealand."

After noting that: "There are still some things that remain over", including remaining grievances, Ngata went on to recognise that all had played a role in the development of the nation, and that all shared the responsibility of each in upholding the treaty, with both successes and failures.

"This gentlemen's agreement called the Treaty of Waitangi on the whole hasn't been badly observed. There are times when we all have a good look at a gentleman to see how on the whole he has behaved and I suppose you *pakehas* look at us and wonder what sort of men we are in fulfilling our obligations under the treaty. ... **This [the Treaty of Waitangi] is the great gift of Her Majesty who said in 1840 'I give to you now the finest gift in my power as the queen of the *pakehas*. I am going to make you equal to the *pakeha*.'** ... If anything brings home to the Maori what complete citizenship of the British Empire means it is that side by side with the privileges of that citizenship go its obligations. Very well, we start the new century with our eyes wide open as to what the obligations are. That is the message of the Maori people to you today. We hope that the *pakeha* will help us to be, and to remain, Maori in the [spirit?] of our culture while reaching forward to the strength in the material things that belong to the *pakeha* in order that we may attain full citizenship – not the same, not identical citizenship, but equal and, as far as it lies in the Maori, to carry out his obligations as a citizen."

This is an important point, which must be considered in today's debate. All share in responsibility, and most, in both groups, had done their best. There is some similarity with the expressions of the chiefs at Kohimarama; both are a celebration of the positive aspects of coming together as one people and a recognition of remaining issues still to be worked through in the long process of forging a unified nation.

Challenges faced; difficulties overcome

The British came with the ideals of equality, a Christianity that emphasised the good of all, and a desire to bring a new humanitarian colonisation, which would refuse to repeat the mistakes of many previous colonial ventures (which they clearly recognised). This was not a conquest by arms but an agreement between two peoples; it did not bring enslavement, but set slaves free.

The formation of this new form of united government was not easy. Many problems arose even when sensible action was taken. This is the law of unintended consequences, where the first aim was successfully achieved but some secondary flow-on effect created a new set of challenges.

The move of the capital from Russell to Auckland, to a more central position, made sense. It also helped to bring peace and resettlement of the Tamaki isthmus. But one immediate consequence was economic downturn in the Bay of Islands, so that many supporters of the Treaty were dismayed that it had brought hardship. Some joined Hone Heke in his dramatic rebellion and the ensuing fighting before being tamed by senior Ngapuhi chiefs and British forces.[102]

So too, the return of freed slaves from Waikato to Taranaki brought conflict, as they found that their ancestral lands had been sold, honestly and properly, by the few struggling survivors there, who had desired the security provided by colonists. Then came others previously driven out, Te Atiawa from Kapiti who now were able to travel through their country free of threats from their former foes, Waikato. They brought with them arguments over land sales, which led to the rebellion at Waitara and subsequent war.

[102102] Robinson 2021

By 1860, there were also growing concerns over the intentions of the burgeoning king movement, many of whose members refused to follow the directives of their peaceful leader, Te Wherowhero.

War did come. When it had concluded, many New Zealanders, settlers and Maori alike, desired to put the past behind them and to move forward together in peaceful co-operation. The goodwill expressed at Kohimarama in 1860 was repeated in the 1878 celebrations of the apparent end of hostility and separatism (sadly undermined the following year when Tawhiao insisted that he was king of a separate state), and again in 1940 when Apirana Ngata spoke of the protection provided by Britain: "That but for the shield of the sovereignty handed over to her majesty and her descendants I doubt whether there would be a free Maori race in New Zealand today."

Other problems were due not to actions but to inactivity, a policy of leaving things alone. This had not been a forceful process of colonisation; Maori remained in control of most aspects of their daily lives, living as before in tribes. Some were unhappy that the early requests to 'give us the law' had not been adequately acted on. That was one of the concerns that led to the formation of the king movement. But the provision of government agents and a nascent legal system in the Waikato was turned back by the more extreme rebels, and development was set back many decades.

Living conditions and general health steadily improved, and the population decline of the pre-1840 period gradually ended, with population growth from 1890 on. The uptake of Western medicine was, however, often slow, both because of Maori fear of diseases within hospitals and the refusal of some chiefs (particularly in the Waikato) to co-operate with the government. Many Maori continued to live in the old way, separate from the newcomers. Inevitably, it took time for the very different cultures to come together.

The hesitant move towards greater integration was reflected in the education system where, despite the success of Te Aute College, the training ground for a generation of important Maori scholars such as Apirana Ngata, most education was in agriculture. The insistence for many years of education in English was a demand of chiefs, with Ngata an enthusiastic supporter: in a 1936 speech that view was strongly stated – if he were allowed to devise a curriculum for the schools, Ngata would make 'English first, second, third, fourth and all the rest of the subjects fifth'. He also advocated a return to a thorough training in English classics in the boarding schools. But, after listening to a new generation of young Maori leaders, he said in 1939 that he had formerly opposed the teaching of Maori in Native schools because he had believed there was not sufficient time for pupils to learn both Maori and English, but that now he believed 'nothing was worse than for one to be with Maori features but without his own language'."[103]

Three essential features of New Zealand history, and the way in which it has recently been rewritten by 'revisionist' historians, have been highlighted in this section on 'Celebrating colonisation'.

1. There is the human story of those actors in the drama; It is truly remarkable how rapidly many Maori chiefs adapted and learned when a new way of life came from across the seas. So many New Zealanders, Maori and British, worked together, eventually succeeding despite problems and conflicts.

2. There was an extraordinary cultural transformation, a revolution within one lifetime. The colonisation of New Zealand brought an inclusive Christianity of genuine concern and love, a desire for equality. This was not the muscular Christianity and the brutal colonisation of a rapacious conqueror, as elsewhere and other times; it was a noble experiment, a glorious exception, that worked. The ideas and beliefs underlying the United Nations Declaration on the Rights of Indigenous Peoples (apart from the

---

[103] Barrington and Beaglehole 1974, pages 204-207; Robinson 2015, pages 141-142.

stirring declaration against racism, which is contradicted throughout the text) are wrong, empty-headed, ignorant, confused nonsense.

3. The true story is now missing from the modern rewrite for political gain, which has been a fight to undo the progress of the past. There is an immense difference between the truth and the modern narrative.

Progress through the twentieth century

Clarity of language, and of thinking, has gone from legislation in New Zealand. The law which guides and directs us – all – is written in a language that is inexplicable, dense and open to multiple interpretations. In much legislation and governance, one chosen group (local *hapu* or *iwi*) has been given the power to interpret legislation and regulation as they wish to determine the meaning of words, to suit sectoral interests, and power is taken from the people and handed to gatekeepers from that chosen group.[104] The confusion that is written into law, the separation and election of specially defined representatives, has destroyed any meaningful democracy.

We are no longer guided by facts, as an imagined (unspecified and mysterious) *tikanga* replaces definite regulations, allows re-interpretation of law by one party, and demands the employment at public expense of many powerful gatekeepers who alone can decide what our laws mean. Nor are events placed into the context of the times (then or now).

There is a widespread refusal to acknowledge historical facts, including the eye-witness accounts of those on the spot, at the time. Instead, prominence is given to invented accounts with the focus on grievance, to the stories told by the rebels only, setting aside the experiences and wishes of majority Maori (as expressed at Kohimarama in 1860).

Some even say there is an unbridgeable gap between cultures that can never be closed, imagining an impenetrable barrier that has been inherited and which continues to this day – when there is so much intermarriage and we all live within a twenty-first century developed society and lifestyle. The reality is a shared way of life.

---

[104] Robinson 2019

It is as if today a person of mixed ancestry (including most, if not all, Maori) must be truly confused – with one part of his or her inheritance and upbringing not able to understand or communicate with the other part. This idea is found in the even more absurd, yet frequently expressed, claim that the culture of *tikanga* is embedded 'in our DNA'. But DNA is entirely inherited and does not change, whereas culture and a way of life do – as shown graphically by the very different attitudes and actions between 1820 and 1840 of warrior chiefs become peacemakers, such as Tamati Waka Nene and Te Wherowhero.

The destruction of meaning in language has become a means of asserting power, a deliberate politic ploy to assert race-based special treatment, with claims of permanent cultural gaps dividing us. The descendants of nineteenth century rebels want to continue to hold apart as a separate people, never forgetting the grievances of defeat.

To dwell on exaggerated grievance is to forget, to set aside, any recognition of the many meetings and shared participation in the development of New Zealand. There have been so many discussions showing true awareness, of the appreciation of the need to come together, and the possibility of understanding one another, from the times of first contact. Some such that stand out include:

- The discussion of Hongi Hika with missionaries before he set off to war – "*Missionaries*: War is a wicked, bad thing. *Hongi: A* bad thing indeed."[105]

- The clear, intelligent speech of Tamati Waka Nene at Waitangi – "What did we do before the *Pakeha* came? We fought, we fought continually. But now we can plant our grounds, and the *Pakeha* will bring plenty of trade to our shores. Then let us keep him here. Let us all be friends together."[106]

---

[105] Robinson 2015, pages 35-43
[106] Robinson 2015, pages 81-82

- The 1857 assent of Governor Gore Browne to a Waikato request for *runangas*, a European magistrate, and laws, met with acclaim. The senior chief, Te Wherowhero, was pleased – "Potatau declared that he would be guided by the Governor's advice. He was a dying man, and should bequeath his people to the Governor's care."[107]

- The many statements of chiefs from across New Zealand in 1860 at Kohimarama when others were threatening war.[108]

This had been a meeting of minds. So, too, were the many deep friendships of Governor (and Premier) Grey with many chiefs, such as Tamati Waka Nene, Te Wherowhero (in 1846 Te Rauparaha was freed into the custody of these two chiefs) and Rewi Maniapoto. In fact, the early and continuing understanding between Maori and Europeans was truly remarkable.

Maori gained considerably from colonisation and the subsequent formation of the independent, self-governing nation of today. But into the twentieth century most still lived largely apart, and did not share all facilities (often by choice), such as hospitals and other health care. This changed with the wartime and post-war move to cities, so that by 1970 a majority of Maori were living in cities, being now close to the non-Maori measure of 80%.

It was then that many Maori became part of the working class, which had been well represented and supported at the time, and they were given considerable assistance by trade unions. Also, Maori gained better access to public facilities, such as schools and hospitals.

---

[107] Robinson 2016, pages 120-121
[108] Robinson 2022

Figure 1. Proportion of Maori and Non-Maori populations living in urban areas

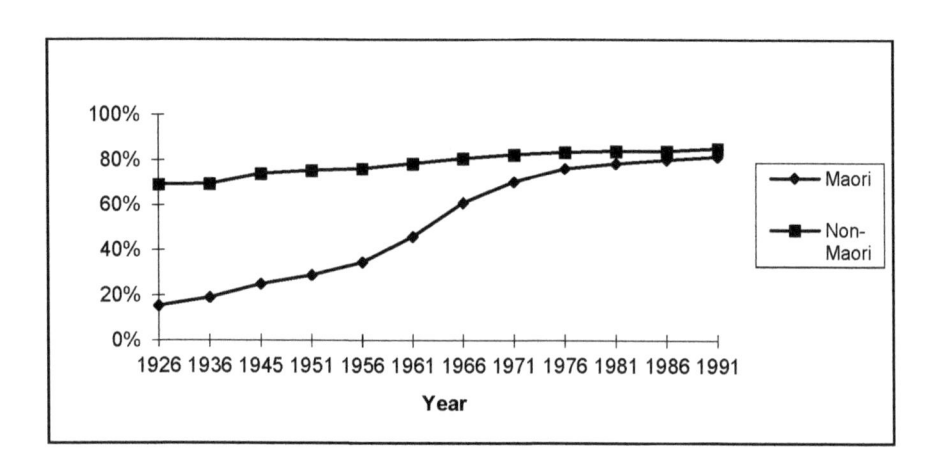

The benefits of integration have been evident, as shown in many measures of healthcare and survival. There has always been high child mortality among undeveloped peoples; in 1885, only half of Maori survived past their 14th birthday (still with high death-rates among non-Maori, with around 85% surviving). With better care and nutrition, that percentage of child deaths steadily reduced over time, so that now less than 1% (of both Maori and non-Maori) die in those early years. That was a success in health, of colonisation.

In the same way, measures of life expectancy at birth have improved, with Maori values steadily converging towards the higher non-Maori values. The previously high difference was becoming far less as this, as with other ethnic gaps, steadily reduced and differences between the two were disappearing. Maori life expectancy before contact would have been 20-25 years.[109] Add in the massive death-toll and social disruption of the musket wars, and **life expectancy must have**

---

[109] author's estimate, based on available demographic information

been **significantly less than 20 years** in the years preceding the Treaty of Waitangi.

Figure 2. Life expectancy at birth, Maori and non-Maori, males and females

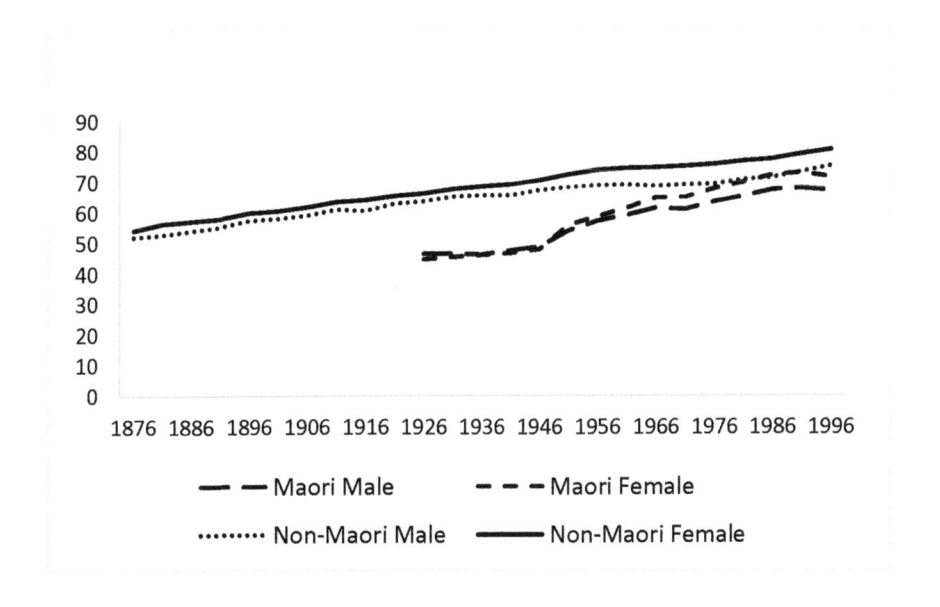

Maori life expectancy had doubled between 1840 and the first half of the twentieth century, but was still 20 years less than non-Maori. The next graph, of the differences in life expectancy, shows the steady reduction in that gap, and the reversal of the trend around 1984 and subsequently when government policies, with a move from import restrictions to free trade and globalisation, brought high unemployment (especially among the young and unskilled) and an upsurge in inequality. Those policies remain basically in place today, and have never been the focus of Maori politicians who concentrate of grievances (largely invented) and separation.

Figure 3. Differences in life expectancy (years) between Maori and non-Maori, for males and females

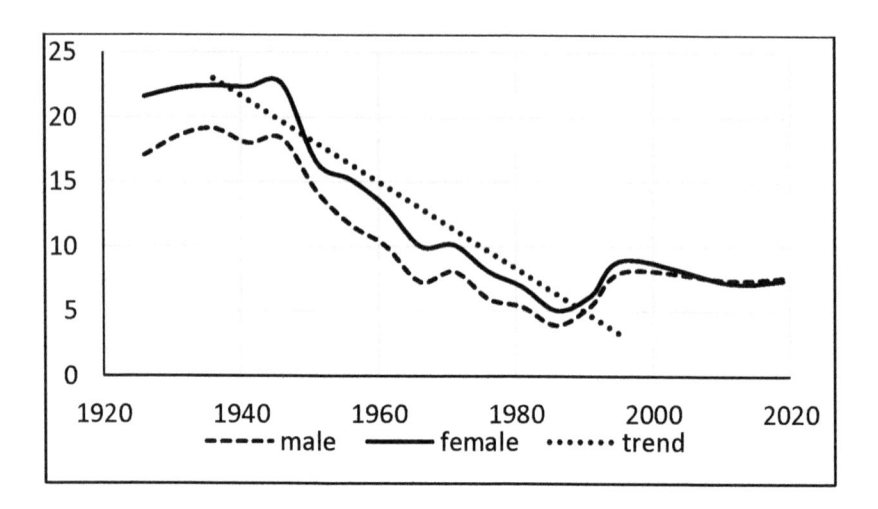

```
25
20
15
10
 5
 0
   1920    1940    1960    1980    2000    2020
         ----- male  ——— female  ······ trend
```

The rapid decrease in the gap between Maori and others is clear. The added, dotted, trend line suggests that the convergence might have been complete by around the year 2000, but the change in trend evident since around 1984 took the gap back up from 5 years to 7-9 years.

Surely an increase in life expectancy for Maori through the years of colonisation and independence, from 20-25 years to 70-75 years today, is an achievement, but the grievance culture leads many Maori to focus only on the remaining gap, never thinking to explore the context and thus failing to recognise that the difference might well have disappeared before now if it had not been for the country's change of direction in 1984 – obviously, nothing to do with the long-past colonisation.

These are just a few of the facts telling of the successes of colonisation and the subsequent national government. We should learn from this experience: integration works, separation (as when Maori had different schooling and lived apart) does not.

PART 2: BUILDING A NATION

Whaling, sealing, timber and construction industries

In the chapter, 'Before Maori: the first settlers', it was noted that New Zealand had long remained uninhabited by man, being the last significant inhabitable landmass on earth to be discovered and settled.

"Pre-European Maori culture belonged to the stone age; the working of metal was unknown and so were pottery, animal husbandry, the bow, and the wheel; weaving, in the proper sense of the word, was not practised. Thus, if one merely lists the number of things the Maori had, the culture seems very impoverished indeed; yet its level was higher than such poverty might make one suppose. To take animal husbandry as only one example; the Polynesians in tropical Oceania did keep pigs as domestic animals. Therefore if the Maoris did not have them it was not because they were too primitive, but because they were unable to bring them to New Zealand. The marked characteristic of Maori culture is that a high degree of technical skill was used to make efficient objects out of the very few materials at hand. Thus, essentially, their clothing was made of leaves, but these leaves were meticulously processed. ... Again, Maori stone tools could be of very high quality and capable of doing many of the jobs of iron tools, though more slowly. Garden culture was very efficient [but labour intensive] in those districts where the sub-tropical Maori-introduced crops could flourish. Boatbuilding and navigation were among the most remarkable of Polynesian skills."[110]

---

[110] Schwimmer 1966, page 10

Pre-European Maori food was gathered from bush, sea, rivers and lakes. Birds, fish, shellfish, eels, vegetation, eggs and wild honey were taken and prepared for eating. They kept dogs for eating; the moa was a major food source for a brief period until it was hunted into extinction.

Some root crops were cultivated. "Living in the extreme south of Polynesia required rather more effort than in the tropical lushness of places like Tahiti. Most of the staple crops of the tropical Pacific were not brought to, or did not survive in, New Zealand. The one staple that did – the sweet potato – required very considerable planning and hard work to enable it to survive. In many parts of New Zealand such as in the southern North Island and most of the South Island a hunting and gathering lifestyle, as opposed to a more sedentary agricultural life, was required." The chewing of fern roots contributed to poor dental health. Life expectancy was poor: "Prehistorians are [in 1984] in the process of painting the now academically respectable view (though one quite at odds with fashionable romantic and political views of the pre-European Maori) of a lifestyle which, in neo-Hobbesian language, is characterised as 'harsh, hungry and short'."[111]

This was all to change with the coming of the British, as Maori began to reconnect with the wider world that had considerably advanced during the long period of separation; the arrival of Cook in 1769 brought the end of isolation.

In the closing decade of the 18th century, sealers and whalers began to arrive in their hundreds seeking to exploit local resources. They came from many nations: mostly Europeans (British, Dutch, French, Russian, German, Spanish and Portuguese), and North Americans (many from the New England whaling ports).[112]

---

[111] Howe 1984, pages 201-202
[112] https://nzhistory.govt.nz/culture/pre-1840-contact/sealers-and-whalers

For some time, sealing and whaling were operated by offshore companies and were largely ship based. The saleable products were skins, bones and oil. But this exploitation of a natural resource was uncontrolled; seals in New Zealand had been hunted to the verge of extinction by 1830 and sealing was outlawed in 1926.[113]

Whalers hunted off the northern coast from about 1794: "The end of the third decade of the century found quite a number of Sydney firms engaged in the sperm whale trade, in company with the whaling vessels of England, Europe, and America."[114] Some Maori joined whaling vessels as crew, and Sydney became the most visited overseas destination for Maori.

Later, some large land-based stations were built. Many shore-based whalers took Maori wives and were referred to as '*Pakeha*-Maori' as they lived with the tribe. Many prominent Maori have that part-European ancestry.

Traders and whalers John Agar (Jacky) Love and Richard (Dicky) Barrett formed an economic relationship with Te Atiawa at New Plymouth in 1828: both men were given Maori names: Barrett's name was transliterated as Tiki Parete, while Love became known as Hakirau. Acceptance into Te Atiawa was sealed through marriage, and their descendants have established 'Love' and 'Barrett' as prominent Maori names. Love was the owner and captain of a whaling boat, *Tohora* (The Whaler) in the late thirties and Barrett was first mate at one time.

When George Stubbs, an Australian-born whaler and trader of English extraction, married a prominent Ngati Toa chieftainess, Metapere Waipunahau, on Kapiti Island, his son took up a Maori name, Wi Parata, which is recognised today in Waikanae. By 1868, Parata had begun farming and by 1875 ran about 1,600 sheep.

---

[113] https://www.doc.govt.nz/our-work/heritage/heritage-topics/sealing-and-whaling/
[114] McNab 1913, pages 1-2

Another was Norwegian Hans Felk, who took on the name Phillip Tapsell ('topsail'). He was working on whaling ships in the 1820s when he came to New Zealand. In 1830, Tapsell settled in Maketu in the Bay of Plenty at the invitation of a Te Arawa chief; he married Hine A Turama, a Ngati Whakaue woman of high rank and they had six children together. In 1837, Phillip Tapsell set up a trading station at Whakatane which employed several other Pakeha-Maori as agents for the sale of flax and muskets. Phillip Tapsell lived among Maori for 50 years; his lasting legacy now includes more than 3,500 descendants.

Such cohabitation with Maori was shared by other early settlers; rather than being totally divided by history and culture, they understood one another and got on well together. Perhaps that was the greatest contribution that they – these men, their wives and the tribes – made to New Zealand: to show that peoples from such very different cultures could live together.

The value of the forests was immediately recognised by the British with the result that another early, pre-Treaty, industry was timber cutting and trading.[115] Around 1815, missionary Rev. Marsden financed his first visits by carrying loads of timber to Australia in the *Active*, and from 1828 at the Wesleyan mission at the richly-forested Hokianga, William White received a commission from timber trading – which earned the ire of his fellow missionaries.

At first, most of the timber trade was carried out by European sawmillers, with much of the felling, hauling and loading of timber done by Maori labour. In 1825, missionaries pointed out to a meeting with a group of chiefs, led by Hongi Hika, that: "The missionaries have already been sufficiently long on shore for many of you to have learnt the civil arts of life such as carpentry, blacksmithing, shipbuilding, reading and writing, etc. ... If you were to sit quiet at home and cultivate your lands and learn the book, you would soon

---

[115] Robinson 2015, pages 36, 40-41

become like us. There is a vessel being built now which would take your articles of trade to Port Jackson [Sydney], where you may dispose of them to good advantage. For instance, if you were to saw timber, the plank would there fetch a good price. If you were to cultivate your lands, in a proper manner which you have now the advantage of doing, you may load the vessel with wheat, which article would also be sure to meet a good market in the Colony. If you were to dress a quantity of flax, this would also fetch a good price."[116]

From 1829, a group of prominent Ngapuhi chiefs, most notably brothers Tamati Waka Nene and Patuone and their cousins, the brothers Te Wharerahi, Rewa, and Moka, aided with the preparation of kauri for shipment and they became traders in their own right.[117] They made a number of trips to Australia: Rewa had been in Sydney in 1830-31 and Patuone was in Sydney on business in 1835.[118]

Several ships had been constructed in New Zealand by 1830, at Horeke in the upper reaches of the Hokianga Harbour.

New Zealand built ships were not entitled to a British register as New Zealand was not a British colony, nor a foreign country with a central government and shipping registry, and so they could not legally trade between New South Wales and the islands under an 1827 British Order in Council. The *Sir George Murray* was seized in 1830 on arrival at Port Jackson, and sold; in 1833 the New South Wales customs authorities seized the *New Zealander*. The British Resident in New Zealand, James Busby, found a solution with the choice of a maritime flag.[119]

---

[116] Robinson 2015, pages 110-111
[117] Davis 1876, page 67
[118] Robinson 2015, pages 58 and 64
[119] Roche 1990, pages 26-28; Sherrin 1890, page 368; Robinson 2015, pages 60-61

In the years following the signing of the Treaty of Waitangi, northern Maori were to learn that, while becoming part of a developed economy involved considerable gains, it also brought unexpected economic problems. The imposition of customs duties in 1840 removed the possibility of charging dues to visiting vessels, and the movement of the capital from the Bay of Islands to Auckland brought reductions in trading opportunities.

Kauri logging was wasteful; Ernest Dieffenbach described the kauri logging as 'a melancholy scene of waste and destruction'. The Royal Navy was concerned with security of supplies and sent a qualified person to assess the forests suitable for naval purposes, and the Governor of New Zealand was instructed to issue timber licences for cutting kauri on 'waste lands' of the Crown. The requirement of a licence for kauri felling impacted considerably on the Ngapuhi business, so that, with the decline of the Hokianga timber trade, the *hapu* involved fell heavily into debt.[120]

The timber industry was to continue to provide a valuable resource for building houses for the growing nation. The use of native timber was steadily replaced by plantations of exotic trees, many planted from 1923 on following research which identified a number of nutrient deficiencies in many New Zealand soils and then the development of treatment processes, so that suitably treated pine could be approved for home building. These efforts included the development of a pulp-and-paper industry.

The wealth of the country was being built by the efforts of many people – of many cultures, from many places, including sailors, whalers and sealers, settlers and traders, timber cutters, carpenters and ship-builders, scientists and businessmen.

---

[120] Robinson 2015, page 110

Missionaries, settlers and farmers

Visiting ships and early settlers brought many new foods to New Zealand. These included domesticated animals such as pigs, sheep, cattle, poultry, and a wide range of vegetables and fruit. The diet of Maori was transformed very much for the better; teeth were no longer worn down by chewing fern roots. Maori soon began to learn the wide range of introduced gardening skills, as well as becoming familiar with new metal tools. Horses came, then coastal and international shipping, followed by roads and rail.

The long period of millennia of isolation was over as Maori were reconnected with the great mass of humanity, learning of and visiting the developed world.

Missionaries were among the first settlers, dedicated to learning of, and understanding, the Maori, to teaching Christianity and the culture of Europe, hoping to improve their lives. After initial discussions and visits, lay preachers sent by the Anglican Church Missionary Society came to Rangihoua in the Bay of Islands in 1815; the Wesleyan Methodist Missionary Society established a mission outpost at Whangaroa in Northland in 1823; Bishop Pompallier celebrated the first Roman Catholic mass at Hokianga in 1838 before settling in the Bay of Islands. Maori converts and preachers, and a growing number of missionaries and priests subsequently spread Christianity across New Zealand. Many Maori were fascinated by the magic of literacy; reading and writing were studied and taken up with enthusiasm.

These were not forceful conquerors; they brought the message of peace and a settled way of life, leading by example rather than by coercion, and persevered with little success over many years until the ravages of war led many Maori to look for a better way to live together.

By 1840, a move from tribalism and war was under way; a great number of Maori were turning to Christianity, which was replacing many aspects of traditional *tikanga*. This was a key factor in the comprehensive Maori cultural transformation, another being the welcome signing of the Treaty of Waitangi.

While many of the first settlers came to buy land and develop farms, others came with another, wide, range of skills and occupations, making up the full range of capabilities to build a nation: builders, farriers, smiths, tradesmen, engineers, labourers, traders, businessmen, accountants, lawyers – and, one could mention, the butcher, the baker, the candle-stick maker – not to forget the teachers, nurses and home-makers – all the people who make up a society. All made their own, various, contributions.

Farmers cleared the land and developed agriculture, to produce goods to be exported and to pay for imports from more highly developed nations. Maori made good use of the capabilities. Although during the pre-1840 tribal wars much of the effort went into growing and trading flax to pay for more muskets, after 1840 the Waikato provided much of the food for Auckland – until the king movement and the war of rebellion cut off contact. When the fighting was over, the warning of land confiscation was acted upon and trained soldiers were settled in the Waikato to provide a readily available military force in case of further insurrection – and, as noted previously, in 1879 Tawhiao refused an offer from Grey to regain the majority of the lost land. A great opportunity for development and advancement on the part of Maori had been lost. Meanwhile, the Waikato was being developed by settler farming into one of the richest areas of New Zealand.

New Zealand has always been a trading nation, far from the centres of manufacturing, and those connections meant that it shared in the economic cycles of Europe and the USA (including the great depression of the 1930s, followed by the Second World War). Farming became the backbone of the economy, providing wool and foods for Great Britain. A range of local manufactures was encouraged: however, the demand for imported goods was so great that in 1938 the Government introduced import and exchange controls. When Britain joined the European Economic Community (EEC) in 1973, a special access arrangement had been made to protect New Zealand dairy sales, but exports to Britain continued to decline and New Zealand developed other markets (such as Japan).

Import controls allowed the expansion of local industries and New Zealand became more self-sufficient (in 1965, exports of goods other than the traditional primary products were 4% of the total figure; in 1985 they amounted to 35%). The increased employment opportunities, including for meat exports, led to a great migration of Maori into the cities during and after the Second World War. Then a major shift in economic activity came in 1985 when remaining protections were removed; there were substantial tariff cuts and the removal of licencing protection.

Many of the jobs lost then had been carried out by Maori, who suffered greatly from the surge of unemployment past the end of the twentieth century, bringing hardship and growing dissatisfaction, from which some are suffering today.

The arrival of Europeans and the establishment of a British colony is today presented as an unmitigated disaster for Maori. This is to forget the long list of benefits, which are briefly outlined here. The early mistake was the setting up of a rival king in the Waikato in 1858, followed by rebellion, which was so feared by chiefs from across the country when they met at Kohimarama in 1860.

The key factor influencing the situations of all New Zealanders within recent times has been the overturn of the economy by 'Rogernomics' in 1984 and the subsequent years (including the following Jim Bolger National Government with its 'Ruthanasia'). The nation moved from a protected, mixed economy to policies of free trade and globalisation.

There are good reasons for unhappiness and disquiet among many New Zealanders, not only Maori. Unfortunately, the cause of present problems is claimed to be wrongs of colonisation, which led to the development of a modern nation, with considerable improvements in the lifestyle of Maori, whereas the driving force has in fact been the more recent change of economic and political direction. A solution should be sought in overcoming those problems, and not in a focus on a false, rewritten story of what was in fact a long-past successful era, which is bringing the destruction of much that was gained and the tearing apart of the nation.

Roads and rail

New Zealand was fortunate in being built almost from scratch at the height of the Industrial Revolution in Britain. The mid to late 1800s were the high point of Britain's wealth and engineering achievements, and virtually all the engineers and contractors who built New Zealand's early infrastructure of roads and bridges, railways and tunnels, viaducts and wharves, tramways and the telegraph, had received their training in Britain, which was known as 'the workshop of the world'. Britain was the richest country in history up to that time and there was plenty of capital on the London market to finance large construction projects in both the British Empire and elsewhere.[121]

The engineers brought to New Zealand not only high standards of design and draughtsmanship but also open and imaginative minds which were needed in this new country of high mountains, raging rivers and challenging terrain, such as the Raurimu Spiral on the North Island Main Trunk railway. Their work was generally of the highest professional standards and we owe a lot to the institutions in Britain that trained them and the engineering firms that gave them their experience before they boarded a smelly, crowded sailing ship for a four to five month voyage to the farthest ends of the earth.

The physical building of the country in only a generation or two from 1840 is one of New Zealand's finest achievements as, when the first settlers arrived, there was virtually nothing in the way of inland communications or public convenience. As Arthur Carman wrote in his book, *Tawa Flat and the Old Porirua Road*, "A notable feature in early pioneer life in these southern wilds was the adaptability and resource of our early settlers. On arriving here they found a savage land covered with dense, primeval forest. They had to discard the

---

[121] McLean 2020b

fruit of nearly all past experience in the task of making a living, and learn to understand and cope with new and strange conditions. ... They entered the dark forest and dwelt in the roughest of 'new chum' camps. ... Their lot was the heavy labour, the aching muscles of the bushman."

In a lecture to the Philosophical Institute of Canterbury on 5th November, 1866, Edward Dobson, Canterbury's Provincial Engineer, said, "With scanty means and a comparatively small population we have succeeded in introducing amongst us most of the great inventions of the civilised world. We have our telegraph through the country, and our submarine cable connecting our capital [Christchurch] with the seat of government in the North Island. We have our great tunnel [Moorhouse] in construction and our road [Otira] across the New Zealand Alps. We have our goldfields, our coal mines, our foundries, our broad acres tilled with the steam plough, our clipper steamers, our mail coaches and our locomotive railways, and we have all this in a country which, fifteen years ago, was an almost unknown land but which is now, with God's blessing, the happy home of prosperous thousands of our fellow men."

The building of the roads transformed inland travel. "The Maori having no animals but the dog, no vehicles, and no sharp-edged tools, his tracks were all footways formed merely by the padding of horny feet and the breaking off by hand of obstructing vegetation".[122] After organised settlement began in 1840 the need for roads between settlements became acute as "the use of traditional Maori tracks and river routes could not meet *Pakeha* needs", foot travel being "vexatiously slow".[123]

The first important road to be built was the Hutt Road, which was dug out of the steep, thickly bushed hillside on the western shore of Wellington harbour to link the settlements of Petone and Wellington

---

[122] Holcroft 1977, page 75
[123] *NZ Herald*, 22 January, 1940

proper. Other roads were hacked through the thick bush such as the one from Kaiwharawhara, on the Hutt Road, up to Porirua harbour, and the Great South Road which led from the centre of Auckland down into the Waikato.

After the end of the native wars the versatile men of the Armed Constabulary, who were stationed at various inland camps in the North Island for peace-keeping purposes, swapped their rifles for the spade and built or helped to build several roads, including that from Hawera to New Plymouth slightly inland from the coast, the road from Tokaanu to Wanganui, the Napier-Taupo road, the one from Taupo to Rotorua and then on to Tauranga and Katikati, from Cambridge to Tirau and then over the Mamaku range to Rotorua, and from Pirongia to Kawhia on the coast. These advanced the settlement of the interior and "showed the hostile Maoris that every part of their country could be reached sooner or later by roads ... In this way the places that were dangerous backblocks were opened up to travellers and pioneer settlers".[124]

When rivers were encountered they had to be bridged, often with a swing-span bridge so that boats were not prevented from passing up river.

The mid nineteenth century was the great age of railways and these too began to spread across the land like a giant spider's web. By 1870 there were only 46 miles of railway in all of New Zealand – on three different gauges. During the next nine years, as a result of the Vogel Public Works policy, another 1,136 new miles of railway were laid.

The two biggest railway building challenges were the North Island Main Trunk railway (completed 1908) and the trans-alpine railway from Christchurch to the West Coast (completed 1923) with the opening of the Otira Tunnel which, at five and a quarter miles in

---

[124] *Auckland Star*, 10 April, 1937

length, was at the time the longest tunnel in the British Empire and the longest tunnel in the world outside the European Alps.

The earlier Moorhouse railway tunnel under the Port Hills had connected Christchurch with its port of Lyttleton while, of the several tunnels on the North Island Main Trunk line, the Poro-o-tarao tunnel, south of Te Kuiti, was by far the most difficult to construct. Supplies had to be sent from Pirongia by barge up the Waipa River and Mangaokewa Stream to a stockpile in Te Kuiti. From there they were taken by sledge or horse over thirty miles of river and swamp and hills to the tunnel site. Dynamite had to be used to clear snags from both the river and the stream. The Main Trunk line required viaducts to be built over steep gorges and inaccessible country, including the Waitete, Makatote and Makohine viaducts.

Ports such as Auckland, Wellington, Lyttelton and Port Chalmers required ever larger wharves extending into deeper water as well as docks for repairing ships after their long voyage from England. Lighthouses were built around the dark and rocky coast, some on land, such as Pencarrow at Wellington, while others rose out of the sea such as the Ponui Passage Lighthouse in the Hauraki Gulf.

Before the age of the telephone, it was the telegraph that was the main means of communication between settlements and wires on poles had to be built all over the country, often alongside railway lines. The first telegraph line was between Christchurch and Lyttelton in 1862 while the most challenging task was laying the submarine cable under Cook Strait in 1866.

All this work – the physical building of the country – was done by the pioneer settlers with virtually no convict labour – as in Australia – and little native labour. It was a remarkable achievement and of enormous benefit to all, including the Maori who no longer had to walk through the bush to get from place to place but could now ride along roads on their horses or take a ride in a train. For example, with the building of the Otira road the Kaiapoi Maoris in their trips to the West Coast for greenstone no longer had to swim across three deep pools in descending the treacherous Otira gorge.

In finally accepting – and then welcoming – the Main Trunk railway through the King Country, Rewi Maniapoto, formerly an adversary of settler progress into the King Country, said, "Tell Mr. Bryce [the Minister of Native Affairs] to hasten on the railway. I am an old man now and I should like to ride in the railway before I die".[125]

A big part of Western civilisation over the years has been providing people with a sustained improvement in the material quality of their lives, and the penetration of roads and railways into the interior brought the amenities and comforts of the advanced world to the back country where too many Maori had been living in squalor, isolated from doctors, hospitals and supplies of healthy food.

---

[125] Fletcher 1978, page 17

Felling kauri

Sir Apirana Ngata leading the haka at Waitangi in 1940 to celebrate the centenary of signing the Treaty.

Products of colonisation. Above: from wild country to vineyards in the Hawkes Bay. Below: the neatly laid out city of Hastings.

New Plymouth, 1860, when it was strongly garrisoned against attack.

The redoubt and garrison at Pukearuhe, Taranaki.

Men of the Armed Constabulary, 1881.

Wool and meat

The first recorded sheep in New Zealand, eight merinos, arrived with Reverend Samuel Marsden in 1814, and by 1824 wool and meat were being produced; the number of sheep became 13 million in 1878, most raised for wool which could be readily exported. This created a problem of what to do with the excess of around 3 million carcases a year, far more than were required in the local market. A few could be canned; some were rendered (to produce fat for candles, etc.) and many were dumped in the sea.[126]

The answer was refrigeration, and in 1882 a sailing ship, the *Dunedin*, took the first consignment of frozen New Zealand mutton to England. This was highly profitable; three more abattoirs were built that year (freezing was initially on the ship), and many more ships came into service (to 71 ships in 1914). Later, freezing works were built on shore (constructed and run by investors, engineers, with a work force having a variety of skills), removing the need for freezing on board the ships, which then required just insulated storage. In the 1970s refrigerated containers were introduced.

Freezing works employed many workers, both skilled and unskilled, and paid them comparatively high wages. In 1927, Gisborne Sheepfarmers Frozen Meat and Mercantile Company, with its large Kaiti works on the Gisborne waterfront, boasted that it was the largest employer of labour and largest distributor of wealth in Poverty Bay; many of the workers were Maori.

The number of sheep, and the employment in the freezing works increased. The First World War was a boom time; by 1930 there were 30 million sheep in New Zealand, and the number reached 70 million (to oversupply the market) with the support to farmers by the

---

[126] Much of the information in this chapter is from a talk to the Kapiti Historical Society by Ian Marsden in April, 2022.

Muldoon government. Then in 1985 the industry was deregulated and subsidies were removed. Large financial institutions bought up much of the industry, including a number of farmer co-operatives. Problems in the industry were further exacerbated by the 1986 financial crash.

The result was a steady and considerable decline in sheep numbers and in freezing works. The number of sheep fell from the maximum of 70 million in 1984 to 30 million in 2010.

Several points are significant here.

- This entire industry, with introduced animals and technology, and improvements based on British science and knowhow, owed nothing to *matauranga Maori* – which is now proclaimed as basic to science in New Zealand.

- Developments of the industry, with employment opportunities for Maori, as for other New Zealanders, was separate from colonisation (other than the settled conditions for the development of that whole industry). The boom times were due to events overseas and to government policies in a self-governing nation with an electorate including all people. Both advances and problems are the consequence of government and industry action through to the present, and, similarly, bear no relation to the past colonisation.

- Many Maori who had worked in freezing works, and on farms became unemployed after 1985; there is the reason for some Maori hardship – again, it must be stressed, not the colonisation that had ended so long ago.

If we are to face up to the problems of today, we must understand the basis of past success and the policy decisions that have resulted in social inequality. A false narrative based on a distorted ideology of wrongs of colonisation will continue to mask the real causes while ignoring the need to develop policies better adapted to the real world of today.

Home comforts

The trade in animal products, which played such an important part in the development of New Zealand, depended on refrigeration and the provision of a reliable supply of electricity. As well as helping to build a modern economy, electricity has transformed our homes and daily life – from the time we wake to turn on the light, listen to the radio or watch television, have a shower, heat water for tea or coffee, and throughout the day. These comforts, which we now take for granted, are the consequence of connection to global civilisation, based on the fruit of many centuries of advances in science and technology in the developed world, and in particular for New Zealand, in Britain.

The first major energy source for New Zealand, from the time of the very first settlement, was wood, from the widespread forests. Then coal was discovered on the West Coast in 1848, and became an important energy resource.[127] By 1878, 162,000 tonnes of coal were produced in New Zealand, being used in industry and to produce gas for lighting and heating in growing cities.

From early days, electricity generation has been principally by hydro schemes. There were also fossil-fuelled stations, which, until the 1950s, were small-scale and usually fuelled by coal or coal by-products, providing electricity to cities yet to be connected to hydro schemes and to provide additional support to such schemes.

The first hydro-electric power station of any significance was built for the Phoenix quartz mine near Skippers Creek in 1886, and the first public electricity supply was in Reefton in 1888, generated by a hydro scheme on the Inangahua River. Initial power schemes were for companies or local communities. During the twentieth century

---

[127] McLauchlan et al 1986, pages 189-192

demand grew very rapidly and collective, government action was taken to plan and provide the far more extensive generation schemes required; this was not by tribal organisation, nor was the national effort blocked by tribal intervention (see below for recent developments).

"The history of planning for electricity supply and the construction of power stations by the government in New Zealand tells us much about our past and reflects the kind of society that has evolved in this country. It demonstrates the profound impact of technological innovation and enterprise in a country as far away as it could be from the centres of such developments in Europe and the United States. ...

The electricity-generating industry is a vital part of the country's economy. Investment in generating plant has from the beginning been a crucial aspect of the government's role in providing an infrastructure. It comprises a substantial proportion of national investment and makes a central contribution to economic development. This in itself has assured the industry of a key role in the economy and in political and philosophical debates about the kind of society we want."[128]

The many schemes, each involving a number of linked power plants, required extensive exploration, planning and co-ordination as a series of government-built dams were built (1932-1983): on the Waikato River, in the headwaters of the Waitaki River, around Tongariro, at Manapouri – with supplies from the two islands linked by the Cook Strait cable in 1965. Geothermal power has been supplied from 1956, and is now around 15% of New Zealand's electricity generation, and there has also been significant electricity generation by oil, coal, and gas.

Many home appliances, such as stoves and washing machines, powered by electricity, have been built in domestical industries. Many New Zealanders had early built a secondary industry sector –

---

[128] Martin 1991 and 1998, page 7

including small local breweries, garment factories, printing works and boot factories, ropemaking and papermaking, woollen weaving mills. Then larger companies were formed, and often flourished with production of domestic gas cookers from 1919, and, later, electric stoves. The introduction of import controls in 1938 further stimulated the growth of manufacturing, and many home appliances were produced in New Zealand; by 1946, 24.8% of the labour force was employed in manufacturing, 21.7% in primary industry.

That abundant energy, and the associated appliances, which are fundamental to our comfortable modern way of life, are independent of *matauranga*. The knowhow is all provided by the recent wave of settlers. Their toil, their loss of life, and their contributions must not be forgotten as the national story is told.

However, the recent application of *tikanga* into law and social organisation would have provided a block to the development of the essential electricity system. In June, 2021, the High Court overturned a previous ruling in a dispute between the Ngati He people of Maungatapu Marae and Transpower on the placing of transmission lines; Ngati He had been trying to get Transpower to remove the transmission lines that hung above their *wahi tapu*, The ruling was that the *iwi* litigant should decide the rules to be followed – "it was not up to any court to decide whether the proposal would have an effect on Ngati He's cultural sites. That decision rested with the *hapu* and their *kaumatua* alone."[129]

In the past disagreements over damming of rivers and placement of transmission lines had been dealt on a national level through debate, litigation and compromise; now a complainant can rewrite the rules.

---

[129] Leonard 2021

Schools, health care, and housing

The focus in the previous chapters has been on construction of the physical infrastructure. This was accompanied by direct actions to care for the people, with teaching, health care and attention to living conditions.

Pre-contact Maori were taught – as were other peoples – within the family, the *whanau* and the community. "A boy accompanied his father to the cultivations, where he learnt to use the digging stick and the planting and digging of crops, or else joining in the hunting and fishing expeditions. He made eel traps and fishing nets, dived for crayfish and fresh-water mussels. At the age of eight or nine such skills were usually already mastered. Likewise, the girls learnt housework, gardening, and the preparing of flax for weaving. ... The Maori child also learnt from his elders the history, geography, religion, arts, and above all the rules of behaviour of his people."[130]

Further learning on the job came as some worked for the newcomers: whalers, sealers, on ships and using new tools for cutting timber, followed by schools for reading, writing and the new religion and way of life provided by missionaries – soon to be joined by many Maori, who passed the new skills and religion on to other *iwi*.

Early schools were organised by religious and local groups, such as the Catholic schools from 1841 and the school for children of Nelson settlers in 1842. Secondary schools followed, including Christ's College, Christchurch (1851), Nelson College (1857), Wanganui Collegiate (1852) and Wellington College (1868). Under the 1852 Constitution Act, education became the responsibility of Provincial Councils, resulting in a very uneven pattern of education.[131]

---

[130] Schwimmer 1966, page 39
[131] McLauchlan et al, page 332

There had been many calls from chiefs for education in the introduced knowledge. While the concept of cautious humanitarian colonisation recommended a respect for existing culture without imposition of introduced ways, Maori were given the opportunity to profit from the growing education system. The 1858 Native Schools Act provided £7,000 a year for the education of Maori children and adults in Maori schools, and in 1867 £4,000 a year to subsidise the costs of land, buildings, books and teachers' salaries for Maori schools; Government was taking responsibility for Maori education from the churches. However, the progress of Maori education was blocked by the wars of rebellion that started in 1860, and some Maori communities kept separate for many years.

The 1877 Education Act established a national system of free, secular and compulsory education at the primary school level. The Act did not apply to Maori children, who could attend the free schools if their parents wanted them to. Primary school education was made compulsory for Maori in 1894.

Provisions were also made for higher education. The University of New Zealand was created by Act of Parliament in 1871 and became the examining and degree-granting body for all New Zealand university institutions. The University of Otago, which opened that year, was followed by colleges in Christchurch (Canterbury College, 1873), Auckland (1883) and Wellington (Victoria University College, 1897).

There was never any bar to participation; all were available to Maori. The major hurdle was the requirement to satisfy entry requirements, to have the adequate grounding, so as to be ready to learn at a higher level.

A major effort to extend Maori education began at Te Aute in 1854, a boarding school supported by a government grant of 4,000 acres, with money for sheep and the erection of buildings; Maori added

3,397 acres for the education of their children.[132] The school struggled and was closed in 1859, but (with government assistance) it reopened in 1872, as soon as handsome new wooden buildings were completed.[133] In 1878, a new headmaster, John Thornton, decided to give the College an academic bias, providing the boys with a sound grounding in the full range of skills required in the developed world.

When the 1906 Royal Commission on the Te Aute and Wanganui School Trusts met to consider an allegation that "the land has not been let by public tender or otherwise to the best advantage", Thornton emphasised the need for Maori education to equal the best – that "Te Aute is what Wanganui and Christ's College are to the Europeans".[134] But the Commission wanted to move the focus of the school away from a comprehensive classical education: "That, having regard to the circumstances of the Maoris, as owners of considerable areas of agricultural and pastoral land, it is necessary to give prominence in the curriculum to manual and technical instruction in agriculture." A great opportunity was lost, and (with the support of many chiefs) Maori education was limited to immediately practical skills for some years.

The importance of a range of skills in Maori society was evident in the troubles of the Maori Councils set up in 1900, which provided for elected councils to undertake a number of local government and health functions; some of the councils got into difficulties, largely due to excessive enthusiasm and to inexperience in accounting.[135]

The success of that academic Te Aute programme in preparing Maori for university and leadership roles was demonstrated by the important part that three such scholars played in New Zealand government, health care, and history: Sir Apirana Ngata (MP 1905-1943, Minister for Maori Development 1928–1934), Sir Peter Buck

---

[132] Robinson 2015, pages 178-185
[133] Porter 1974, page 604
[134] Royal Commission 1906; Robinson 2015, pages 219-222
[135] Robinson 2015, page 213

(Te Rangihoa: doctor and medical officer, MP 1909-1914, anthropologist and director of the Bishop Museum, Hawaii) and Dr. Maui Pomare (MP 1911-1930, Minister of Health 1923–1926). All worked hard to improve Maori living conditions.

One such initiative was the passage of the Tohunga Suppression Act in 1907, which was an occasion of celebration for all four Maori MPs, who were united on this issue. The negative impact of the activities of *tohunga* was widely recognised; this Act answered a deep-felt need and was the culmination of many debates and calls for action from Maori chiefs, and including the intervention of Ngata and others at conferences of the Te Aute College Students Association (TACSA).

The widespread concern with the state of Maori hygiene and the unsanitary conditions in villages led many of the better educated Maori to become doctors (such as Pomare and Buck). They were critical of injurious customs and meetings deemed to be useless; the close proximity of many meetings, and the poorly ventilated meeting and sleeping houses, contributed to the spread of infectious diseases. When Pomare became Maori Medical Officer in 1901, he travelled widely, inspecting water supplies and sanitary arrangements, and advising the Maori Councils.

Many of the habits were primitive; in traditional Maori hilltop *pa*, *paepae* (latrines) were located on the side of the hill so human waste would fall well away from living and eating areas. That system was, apparently, not universal. When Dr. O'Carroll was sent by the Government to Parihaka in 1884, he "observed human, pig and dog excrement as high as one's instep".[136]

Yet today *tikanga* is called upon as a guide to modern treatment of wastes, as in the current Three Waters proposals, where the controlling body is to be dominated by Maori – chosen by race – and not by professionals, chosen for their expertise. **There is no**

---

[136] *South Canterbury Times*, 1 November 1884; McLean 2020a, page 77

traditional Maori knowledge or scientific systems dealing with sewage treatment plants or adequate water supply systems for cities.

The dangers of such an approach have been shown by the development of a sewage scheme for Wellington City. A first (and the most inexpensive) proposal, favoured by the engineers, was for partial treatment of sewage, which would then be carried out to sea through a pipeline a kilometre or so, where it would be rapidly diluted and dispersed. This process had been shown to be no threat to fish and the environment.

But Maori spokesmen complained that **any** dumping of human waste in the sea was contrary to *tikanga* – thinking of toilets placed on beaches or the rocks, not of waste treatment with purification plants as required with greater conurbations of people. A more complex, and expensive, scheme was then derived. The city's sewage was pumped 9 kilometres from the wastewater treatment plant at Moa Point (near Wellington Airport) to the Carey's Gully sludge dewatering plant at the Southern Landfill (near Happy Valley). The solid waste was then mixed with green waste (plant materials) at the Living Earth commercial facility to provide useful compost.

That sounded clean and green, but it did not work that way. When I was active in the Stop the Stench group in 2007, a foul stench had been blowing across several suburbs (principally Brooklyn) from the southern landfill for more than twelve years. It was evident that the stench would be stronger at source (in the tip) and that council staff knew what the problem was, yet they pleaded ignorance and refused action until two angry public meetings and a well-signed petition forced their hand. Living Earth was then shut down, and a temporary solution was to bury the sewage sludge (about 45 tonnes of solids per day) in the landfill.

Too many of the recent generation of civic leaders have failed to sustain and improve the basic infrastructure of the nation; this has certainly been true of Wellington. That temporary solution continues today, and in 2021 Wellington City Council budgeted between $147 million and $208 million to find an alternative to the current method of dealing with human wastes.

The result of Maori cultural involvement in wastewater treatment was to block a sensible proposal – *tikanga* was irrelevant and harmful, and the insistence on such a control over the national systems, as in the Three Waters proposal, is foolish. Rather, New Zealand should rely on the science and professional expertise, the educated engineers, who built a modern nation – and stop division by race.

British health care in the nineteenth century was largely a mix of private and charitable, with limited provision by government; there was a danger that Maori, living mostly outside the cash economy, would miss out. In 1846, "Governor Grey obtained money from the British Government to build public hospitals in Auckland, Taranaki, Wanganui and Wellington, primarily for Maoris and for sick and destitute Europeans." In 1885, The Hospitals and Charitable Institutions Act provided for a government subsidy to match voluntary contributions or local rates.[137] As noted above, in 1901 Pomare became Maori Medical Officer, and in 1920 Buck became the first director of the Division of Maori Hygiene in the Health Department.

It was only in 1938 that the Social Security Act provided for free universal hospital care. The intention was to provide also free medical services, but opposition from the doctors' organisation, the New Zealand branch of the British Medical Association, prevented the full implementation.

In the early twentieth century, most Maori were still living apart from the newcomers, with limited modern health care (although much was done by various organisations); many were suspicious of Western medicine and of hospitals, and were reluctant to accept medical care

---

[137] McLauchlan et al, page 310

or hospital treatment. In particular, followers of the king movement in the Waikato had remained aloof from the rest of New Zealand, refusing any part in the struggle of World War I.

The insistence on isolation and separate development continued to cause problems, providing a barrier to government initiatives, and in the late 1920s, standards of health in Waikato were little better than they had been twenty years earlier. Tribal leader Te Puea intended to use a new meeting house (Mahinarangi) as a hospital, but private hospitals had to be licensed and Mahinarangi did not meet the required criteria. The insistence on separation was to continue; the king claimed that he held a unique position, above the law, and he refused to register under the conditions of the 1938 Social Security Act. For these people the lack of advancement was forced by tribal action, not by any government failing.[138]

Health and living conditions improved considerably since Maori isolation ended, when they rejoined the wider world and became integrated into modern society. Those advances continued at a more rapid pace in the period after the Second World War when the previous slow drift of Maori to the cities became a flood (shown in figure 1).[139]

Many social measures continued a steady improvement. As already stated, Maori life expectancy at birth, which had been around 25 years before contact, had improved somewhat to 30 years for women and 35 years for men in 1901. It then increased at an almost constant rate to 77.1 years for women and 73.4 years for men in 2019. The infant mortality rate had been around 500 per 1,000 pre-contact and throughout much of the nineteenth century. The rate declined throughout the twentieth century, to 24.4 per 1,000 in 1971 and 6.8 per 1,000 in 2011, then reducing further in 2018 to 4.9 per 1,000 (to below the 2011 value for the total population of 5.1 per 1,000).

---

[138] Robinson 2015, pages 243-244
[139] Robinson 2012, pages 232-237

Yet, despite the facts, which show how the previous set-up was continually improving the well-being of Maori, the health system has now been broken apart into two separate race-defined organisations.

The move to the cities was a considerable culture shift, as many Maori left communal rural ways behind and joined in the city lifestyle, both striving to adapt and sharing the benefits of better housing, education and healthcare. The collective state provided those facilities. Voluntary groups, and in particular trade unions, provided a further helping hand. The construction of state housing, for all New Zealanders, accelerated from 1936 on, continuing through and after the war.

Throughout the past 182 years (to 2022), integration has brought convergence; Maori living conditions, health, education and housing have improved as we have worked together as one people – until recently, with the push towards separate development, as in education. There is now one curriculum for English medium schools, a second and very different curriculum (with a different message and understanding of the country) for Maori medium schools (*Te Marautanga o Aotearoa*, launched in 2007).[140]

The Three Waters proposal aims to take away local control of water systems, including sewage, with a national system dominated by Maori, with half of the four controlling agencies nominated by *iwi*. It is not at all clear how this will be done, or who will have the power to make these appointments. The Bill only specifies "a regional representative group, which provides joint oversight of an entity by an equal number of representatives of the territorial authority owners and *mana whenua* from within the entity's service area". Perhaps this will be a tribal elite ruling under the claims of *rangatiratanga*, far from any concept of democracy.

---

[140] Robinson 2021, pages 118-127

"The whole system is guided by Maori. The 'dedicated water services regulator for *Aotearoa*', *Taumata Arowai*, which became a new Crown entity in March 2021, 'will operate from a *te ao Maori* perspective aspiring to higher outcomes for *wai* and *tangata* in *Aotearoa*. We will work in partnership across *Aotearoa*, taking our lead from *Te Tiriti o Waitangi*, to regulate and influence the water services sector to improve outcomes and reflect on the importance and interconnectivity of the health of *tangata* and of *wai*. ... *Taumata Arowai* is born out of *Te Mana o te Wai*'[141] (an indigenous perspective on rivers and river management, where rivers, lakes, streams, and springs have been described as the bloodways of *Papatuanuku*, earth mother), working in service of and framed by it as the *korowai* [a traditional woven Maori cloak, symbolic of leadership] for structural and system reform."[142]

That regulator will be directed by *Te Puna* (the Maori Advisory Group), which is chaired by Nanaia Mahuta's younger sister, Tipa Mahuta – an obvious political appointment, keeping control in the family (*whakapapa*, nepotism).[143]

There is never any explanation of why *tikanga* – with a '*te ao Maori* perspective' – would provide better guidance for a modern, developed fresh water and sewage system than the expertise of modern science and engineering. Certainly, the old ways of pre-contact Maori provide no guidance for a suitable modern system.

There are similar questions with the Maori Health Authority set up in 2021 – "developing the locality model of primary and community care in certain areas, some of which will take an approach centred on *kaupapa Maori* care" and "services grounded in *te ao Maori*". That possible turn away from modern medicine rings alarm bells.

---

[141] *Taumata Arowai* information website
[142] Robinson 2021, pages 134-139
[143] https://www.taumataarowai.govt.nz/about/our-team/maori-advisory-group/

Inclusion of *tikanga* (one of three key areas of *te ao*) suggests the reintroduction of old practices. It makes no sense.[144]

Better education, health care and housing came with the new wave of immigrants, a great advance on traditional Maori *tikanga*.

---

[144] Robinson 2021, pages 128-133

Science and knowledge

Early immigrants coming from Britain and other parts of the linked, developed world, were coming to a new and unfamiliar world. They were open to the excitement of discovery, with a readiness to try out something new, to adapt. Such readiness to think anew, to sort out problems, became a feature of New Zealanders.

This continues today in those areas where independent thought is not controlled. When the Ministry of Economic Development (MED) conducted a Business Practice Survey (BPS) in 2001, they found a high level of technological innovation activity, which was surprising to them given the low levels of research and development (R&D) in New Zealand. I carried out a follow-up study which validated those unexpected conclusions: the overall level of innovations was 87%, even greater than the previous 80%, and significantly higher than reported in other countries.[145] New Zealand businesses are less likely to carry out identifiable R&D but more likely to innovate than European businesses. This picture accords well with the popular image of high New Zealand initiative coupled with a low level of formal research activity.

Informal groups to share scientific information began even before ships reached New Zealand. When James Hector came to New Zealand in 1862 to carry out a Geological Survey of Otago, he became an indispensable advisor to government on science, technology, medicine and commerce. He started the colonial museum and laboratory, observatory, and meteorological department. In 1867, Hector, with the help of William Travers MP, set up the New Zealand Institute (via an Act of Parliament) for the study of science, art, philosophy and literature. The name was changed to the Royal Society of New Zealand (RSNZ) in 1933 with a focus on science

---

[145] Robinson 2002

(1965 Act), social sciences, technology and humanities (2012 update to the Act).[146]

For many years the RSNZ was a champion for unfettered science. This has changed. Their rules (the Royal Society of New Zealand Act 1997, amended 2021 by the Council of the Royal Society of New Zealand *Te Aparangi*) now include a "Bicultural Commitment: In giving effect to the objects for which the Society is established, the Society shall encourage policies and practices that reflect New Zealand's cultural diversity and shall, in particular, have due regard to the provisions of, and to the spirit and intent of, *Te Tiriti o Waitangi* (the Treaty of Waitangi)."[147] Such 'spirit and intent' has come to imply a recognition of ancient *tikanga* and *matauranga Maori*, and that commitment to the reformulated Treaty announces a move away from the very basis of independent science to oversight by a totally inappropriate culture. The RSNZ Code of Ethics also instructs that "the application of knowledge conforms to standards acceptable to the wider community", and the RSNZ has a policy, "Vision *Matauranga*, to unlock the innovation potential of Maori knowledge, resources and people."

The development of universities has been mentioned above, including the successful attainment of high standards, which was shown many times, as when Rutherford graduated from Canterbury University College in 1894 before heading overseas, where he continued an illustrious career.

The major scientific establishment, recognising the importance of engineering and science to the nation, has been the Department of Scientific and Industrial Research (DSIR), developing appropriate science and applying it to practical development, with advice to many government departments. The DSIR was set up in 1926 under the guidance of the Permanent Secretary, Ernest Marsden, a physicist

---

[146] https://www.royalsociety.org.nz/who-we-are/our-history/
[147] https://www.royalsociety.org.nz/who-we-are/our-rules-and-codes/general-rules/

who had studied under Rutherford at the University of Manchester. The key to the success of the DSIR was the requirement that science was in the hands of scientists, and the scientific community assigned its own priorities. This is the 'Haldane Principle', calling for the separation of research from administrative departmental control, that guided the early 1920s formation of scientific establishments across the Commonwealth.[148]

That understanding of true science, and the guiding Haldane principle, was ignored in 1992 when the DSIR was closed to be replaced by a number of Crown Research Institutes (CRIs), organised on a commercial mode. Cabinet Minister Maurice Williamson was scathing in his reference to the DSIR: "Well the old DSIR was an appallingly old sort of soviet-style bloc that had less accountability in management than anything I've ever seen. I think the new crown research institutes, which have to bid for their money, along with private sector research people, and along with universities, are the way to go."

The science budget was "going commercial" with the focus on "linking science with business". Funding was controlled by the new Foundation of Research, Science and Technology (FoRST), with the mission of "Actively growing value for New Zealand by investing for results from research and development". The whole new bureaucratic and centralised system was a mess; I recall the director of one CRI telling how they had received funding for the first and third stages of a project but not for the necessary second stage. Control was passing from scientists to chief executive officers with MBA degrees.

Like the RSNZ, the current Ministry of Business, Innovation and Employment is guided by *matauranga Maori*, based on four themes of "indigenous innovation, *taiao, hauora/oranga*, and *matauranga*", which are to provide a powerful framework for considering the

---

[148] Galbreath 1998, page 27

outcomes we expect from Research, Science and Innovation systems (RSI) as they relate to *Te Ao Maori*.[149] The RSI, which they fund, is all-inclusive and refers to "our research, science and innovation system which consists of people, institutions (including research organisations and businesses) and infrastructure."

It is difficult to find the meaning of this. It seems that modern research is to be directed by the pre-contact culture of a tribal society: *matauranga Maori* is traditional Maori knowledge, *hauora* is a Maori view of health, *te ao Maori* is the Maori worldview.

The assertion of that dogma is inimical to science. The unhindered questioning of research under the control of the scientists who understood their own enterprise was replaced by a commercial model, where research is overseen by chief executive officers (CEOs) who were responsible above all for implementing existing plans and policies, improving the company's financial strength, supporting ongoing digital business transformation and setting future strategy – while following directions from a pre-scientific age.

Why had the Haldane principle – now overturned – been so important to scientists? What is the basis of science? What are its core, fundamental principles?

Knowledge, understanding and knowhow had developed internationally over several millennia in many diverse civilisations across the vast Eurasian continent, from Europe in the west to China and Japan in the east, together with Egypt and India to the south, linked and exchanging information through great trade routes and exchanges of scholars. Together those peoples shared the knowledge of metals and mathematics, animals and plants, philosophy and laws, cities and civilisations, reading and writing.

---

[149] https://www.mbie.govt.nz/dmsdocument/6935-new-zealands-research-science-and-innovation-strategy-draft-for-consultation

Progress was steady, but slow, with thinking most often restricted by imposed worldviews, religions and political control. The key modern advance began when scholars in Europe were able to escape from a religious belief in old biblical myths and the interdictions of the Pope in Rome. This was a long process; here are a few milestones of the struggle.

There was an expansion of European navigation and exploration in the late fifteenth century and early sixteenth century: Columbus discovered the Americas in 1492, and in 1522 the survivor of Magellan's five ships returned to Spain after a circumnavigation of the globe. Here was a practical proof that the earth is spherical.

A great leap forward commenced with the Reformation which eventually broke the power of the Catholic Church and the acceptance that the Pope could pronounce that the sun and stars went round the earth, as set down in ancient scripture. The Protestant Reformation had begun around the same time as the global voyages of discovery, in Wittenberg (Germany) when, on October 31, 1517, Martin Luther, a teacher and a monk, published a document he called Disputation on the Power of Indulgences, or 95 Theses.

Another challenge to the power of the popes came in 1534 when Henry VIII created a separate Church of England, to initiate the English Reformation.

The Catholic Church dug in with the brutal Inquisition. When Giordano Bruno and Galileo Galilei dared to believe that the universe was heliocentric, the boundaries that they crossed led to life-changing conflicts with the Catholic Church. In the Copernican system of the universe, the earth rotates on its axis once every day and orbits around the sun every year, contradicting the biblical picture of the earth as centre of the universe. Bruno was persecuted and burnt at the stake in 1600. Galileo was questioned by the Inquisition and was required to recite a formal abjuration; his book was banned and he was sentenced to house arrest until his death.

It was very different in England, as shown by the work of Frances Bacon in the same period, the early seventeenth century. His stress on inductive methods gave a considerable impetus to subsequent scientific investigation. Later that century, Isaac Newton developed a comprehensive system, 'Newtonian mechanics', exploring the laws governing familiar, everyday movement – which are basic to much engineering. There can be no more dramatic example of the difference between freedom of thought and control by a powerful central agency.

The loosening of the strings had allowed a considerable increase in understanding, followed by a further impetus from the eighteenth-century British Age of Enlightenment. The resultant increase in understanding of the world, the new capabilities and technologies, have completely transformed our lives – including advances in life expectancy, travel capabilities, household comfort and business enterprises, the new technologies. The many benefits are now basic features of our civilisation.

That was the birth of modern science, with a methodology of hypothesis and test. The guiding light was experience and observed fact, not myths from the past. The growth of scientific knowledge occurs through challenge to accepted dogma, by "the repeated overthrow of scientific theories and their replacement by better and more satisfactory ones"; the research must not be constrained by insistence on conformity.[150]

This is not the work of an accountant, following set rules: progress so often comes when an accepted idea or hypothesis is overturned – hence the Haldane principle followed by the scientists who understood their craft when they built the DSIR. Those new conditions, and autocratic central control, when the DSIR was disbanded, spelled the end of independent science.

---

[150] Bronowski 1977, page 94, quoting Popper 1959; Robinson 2013, pages 127-128

If I have seen further, it is by standing on the shoulders of giants.
Isaac Newton, 1675

Maori did not stand on those shoulders as the British did. Due to the millennia of separation as Polynesians moved across the Pacific, Maori had missed out on that development – not because they were a fundamentally different people but simply because of that isolation. *Matauranga* has no relationship to science at all; indeed, *tikanga* and *matauranga* lack the basic tools of literacy and mathematics. The world of science has come to include an astonishing range of discoveries – consider the puzzles of alchemy and the scope of chemistry, of electro-magnetism theory and the many applications, of nuclear theory. A list of subjects studied in a typical scientific career (my own) ranged across geometry and calculus to oceanography and computer modelling.[151]

The centuries of scientific achievements came from the escape from superstition, from ancient myths, from an old mystical ideology. The return to this straightjacket, and acceptance of tribal culture, is the second fatal blow in the death of science in New Zealand (following the destruction of the non-commercial DSIR).

We are surrounded by the benefits of the knowledge and goods brought by colonisation since the first contact – they determine every aspect of our lives, with little (if any) derived from *tikanga*. Yet the current idea is to move down from those shoulders, to set aside the wisdom of past millennia gathered together from across the vast Eurasian continent, and then, somehow, to progress in this modern age, driven by the beliefs of an isolated tribal culture, lacking all that immense knowledge built up over so many centuries.

---

[151] Robinson 2021, page 157monitor

Science cannot flourish without the necessary freedom; it will die if scientists are required to bow down before any dogma, any imposed worldview, whatever that may be. The idea that science should be directed by an ancient culture which lacked any of those millennia of information and had no knowledge of the scientific method, together with a treaty that is now torn apart with conflicting versions, is absurd. Research controlled by dogma and instructed by a treaty is no longer science. The scientific enterprise, built by so many wise scholars and which has proved its value, is being destroyed. There is a madness afoot when supposed science is ruled by people who have no understanding of the fundamentals of science.

A proud story

The men and women who became New Zealanders came from all over the world, from different backgrounds, with different talents – first from Polynesia, joined by further immigrants such as the English, Scottish, Irish, Dalmatians, Swedish, Chinese, and many others. They worked together: traders, farmers, missionaries, teachers, engineers, ship-builders and sailors, doctors and nurses, labourers, police, council staff, central government workers, banking staff – the list goes on – to build our nation. The results are all around us, the towns and cities, the electricity and water to our homes, the roads and railways, the shops, tradesmen, everything making up daily life. New Zealand was formed as one people; this our land, for all of us, not as two people separated by race with the two disparate groups in partnership, but together as one. There is so much to remember, with gratitude for what has been achieved by so many, including those who volunteered and served their country in two world wars this past century.

Many conditions have improved since the beginning in 1840; for example, we have a more inclusive democracy, with votes for women and universal suffrage – no longer limited to those with property or wealth. The country is linked by modern communications, and with the move to cities we have come to live more together, less isolated.

It's a great story, to be proud of and to celebrate. This was not the colonisation of elsewhere.

- Not bringing slavery but freedom.
- Not bringing war but peace and security.
- Not conquest but coming in friendship, answering a call for help.
- Not bringing racism but equality.

- Not bringing demographic collapse of the natives but recovery and then growth of population.

All New Zealanders have been working together, to build a nation, with a continually improving democracy, one of the best in the world.

The group that benefitted most were Maori, **with a life expectancy that has more than tripled from 1840 to today**, security rather than constant warfare, equality replacing chiefly dominance, end to slavery, better lifestyle (housing, health care, education) – who so often intermarried with the others: there was never a race bar as people came to live together and work together.

While Maori have joined in, and played their part in the building of the nation, the old culture and the knowhow of tribal society have played no part. It is nonsense now to insist that *tikanga* and *matauranga Maori* should be a governing agent.

PART 3: DESTROYING DEMOCRACY

The Waitangi Tribunal

The Waitangi Tribunal was set up in 1975 as a permanent commission of inquiry charged with making recommendations on claims brought by Maori relating to actions or omissions of the Crown that have potentially breached the promises made in the Treaty of Waitangi. The existence of the Tribunal is predicated on a belief that significant harmful wrong has been done to Maori. The Tribunal's mandate is "to measure prejudice arising from past Crown actions"[152]. Any approach to the Tribunal, with a request to consider and put right perceived wrongs of the past, can be by Maori only.

This had the support of liberal thinkers, such as many in the Labour Government at that time. The dominant perception, at a time when many former colonies had become independent, was that such peoples had been badly treated; there was a widespread desire to put right any wrongs of the past, often with ignorance of particular features of each situation, as if New Zealand has been anything like the Belgian Congo.

The scope was considerably widened in the 1985 Treaty of Waitangi Amendment Act (again a Labour Government) to extend the Tribunal's jurisdiction to historical claims of earlier 'injustices' all the way back to 1840.

The activities of the Tribunal have expanded, with its considerable income and influence. Many (lawyers, researchers, academics and

---

[152] Byrnes 2004, page 188; Robinson, 'The Waitangi Tribunal', Barr et al 2015, pages 144-176

others) have forged successful careers by conformity with the aim to find wrongs of colonisation, continuing to the present time. There are even considerable efforts to manufacture new complaints.

One example is the support material provided to a number of *hui* held in Kapiti, discussing many aspects of the future of the region, where only Maori could speak. A very long list of suggestions of grievances for the *iwi* to consider were set out in the 'Ngatiawa/Te Ati Awa Research Needs Scoping Report 2016'[153], with over 12 pages of bullet points making suggestions for complaints and ground for settlements, in case the local *iwi* had not thought of them. Many were ridiculous, such as: "What was the impact of environmental transformation and management practices on *karanga*, birthing and weaving practices of *wahine* Maori?" That 189-page document proposes considerable further research: a 52-week oral and traditional history project (1 historian, 1 researcher), a 52-week 19th century land issues and Crown relationship report (1 historian, 1 researcher) and a 26-week 20th century overview and gap-filling report (1 co-ordinator). Plus much more, to be paid for by the Crown Forestry Trust, and all to build a case for money and privilege to be handed out from the people of New Zealand (referred to as 'the Crown').

This is just one small region, of so many across the country as the sense of grievance and demands for recompense and special treatment have been nurtured by the well-funded Tribunal and its associated organisations (including the Crown Forestry Rental Trust, which 'provides funding [from annual rental fees for licences to use certain Crown forest licensed lands] to eligible Maori claimants to prepare, present and negotiate claims against the Crown', and which

---

[153] WAI 2200 #A186), available online at http://teatiawakikapiti.co.nz/wp-content/uploads/2016/01/Ng%C4%81tiawa-Te-%C4%80ti-Awa-Research-needs-Scoping-Report-as-at-18-January-2016.pdf.

disbursed $223,368,040 to claimants in 1990-2021[154]). Money is provided by the people of New Zealand to fund cases against the people of New Zealand, and very little is done to develop counter arguments (as would be the case in a fair court of law) or to support the Crown case.

The process has been designed to create permanent grievance. This stands in stark contrast with the South African Truth and Reconciliation Commission, which existed for just five years (1995-2000) as "a necessary exercise to enable South Africans to come to terms with their past on a morally accepted basis and to advance the cause of reconciliation." The Waitangi Tribunal has been growing for forty-seven years (from 1975, now to 2022) and continues stronger than ever, so that New Zealand is more divided than before, with an ever-widening range of grievances and demands for a complete division of government. South Africa got rid of the evils of apartheid; New Zealand is building apartheid.[155]

While the Waitangi Tribunal has been busy extending its scope, the list of settlements decided by the Minister of Treaty Settlements and rubber-stamped by Parliament has continued to grow, building a belief in separate entitlement and supporting the increasing tribal power bases from which *iwi* can push for more division.

In the 2013 edition of *Twisting the Treaty*, there were 32 pages listing settlements, with a total of $1,586.53 million payments for those completed.[156] Five years later, in the revised edition, the list ran to 46 pages, with an expanded total of $3,330.62 million payments for those so far completed. And the end is not in sight. The rulings of the Tribunal, and the subsequent settlements, involve far more than those monetary payments, as shown by a 12-page list of some (98) of

---

[154] https://cfrt.org.nz/wp/wp-content/uploads/2021/08/CFRT-Claimant-Disbursements-2021.pdf
[155] Robinson, 'The Waitangi Tribunal', Barr et al 2015, pages 150-151
[156] Robinson et al 2013

the many Acts of Parliament (up to 2017) giving special rights for Maori.[157]

We must never forget that all these settlements and special rights are taken from us all, with payments from the public purse; we are all paying.

These settlements are not decided within a justice system (a system of equal justice) with defined principles and laws but behind closed doors, in secret agreements to satisfy political aims, without any democratic right of challenge. Information is not made available as these discussions are held to be negotiations between the two parties only, the *iwi* concerned and the 'Crown' (something above us all, not considered to be the people of New Zealand), which in this case is the Minister for Treaty Settlements.

This is far from a neutral fact-finding commission. Waitangi Tribunal hearings are a one-sided affair. When I appeared to talk of my butchered report (referred to below), the meeting room was packed with intimidating Maori and the 'Crown' (us) was represented by two overwhelmed junior lawyers who kept their heads down, while I was questioned arrogantly by several lawyers acting on behalf of Maori claimants, who tried to make mincemeat of whatever I said. That was a totally biased procedure; the aim was to bully me into submission, not to get to the truth.

There is no oversight, no guidelines, no effective representation of the people against the claimant group, often no reasons given (with the grounds for a claim left undefined until an agreement is reached). Whatever the Minister decides is then rammed through by a subservient parliament with MPs happy to feel good with their good deeds to 'indigenous' people, providing recompense for past wrongs,

---

[157] Robinson 2019, Appendix; 1Law4All booklet, *Are we being conned by the Treaty Industry?*, pages 13-26

and joining a global fight to correction of supposed past wrongs of colonisation, a leading nation in a crazy world.

I followed this process closely in the 2010 settlement with Ngati Toa, from the information that the historical account on which the claim was based did not exist while negotiations were ongoing to the final one chance of a submission to the Maori Affairs Select Committee, which was treated with contempt. There was never any real breach of the Treaty, yet Ngati Toa was given around $66 million in cash and properties (including $10 million 'in recognition of Ngati Toa's former marine empire' – the ability to cross Cook Strait and massacre South Island *iwi*) together with special rights over much of the coast (taking those rights from all other New Zealanders).[158]

The whole set-up is simplistic and one-dimensional. The benefits of colonisation, bringing peace and security, the introduction of a national government and the rule of law to replace tribal anarchy, are not considered. Wrongs done by Maori to Maori are ignored. Harm to anyone of European descent, by either Maori or Government, is ignored. A person of mixed blood may complain on behalf of Maori ancestors for some supposed wrong committed by his own European ancestors, and be compensated.

The nineteenth century wars arose from disputes between Maori, rather than action by the government; but this is all too often ignored. As we have seen, these include:

- Arguments between Teira and Kingi, and others, were the basis for feuds and gang warfare that led to many deaths in Taranaki and then the outbreak of war when Kingi refused to accept a legal judgement.

- Many in the Waikato refused to accept a Maori king, while others went ahead with that foolishness by appointing senior chief, Te Wherowhero, as a second monarch for the country.

---

[158] Robinson 2011, pages 29-33

- Te Wherowhero as king told 'his people' not to fight alongside Kingi but Rewi Maniapoto and others went ahead.

- So too, when the second 'king', Tawhiao, ruled that the British agent, John Gorst (who had previously been warmly welcomed by Te Wherowhero), should be left to carry out his work in peace, Rewi Maniapoto drove him out, an action that helped to precipitate war.

There were many murderous attacks on peaceful Maori and settlers, which are not included among the grievances considered – such as the December, 1868, massacre of 30 settlers and 37 Maori at Matawhero in Poverty Bay by Te Kooti.

Those who fought in rebellion broke the Treaty more surely than any action of the Crown – Hone Heke, Wiremu Kingi, the kingite movement, Te Kooti, and others. Those Maori broke the Treaty, broke the law. It would be wise to refuse to dwell overmuch on past offences; they are part of history but not something to require present-day recompense. That should hold for all of us, and the disruptive focus on supposed harm to Maori when so much has been achieved should cease.

Meanwhile, a great deal of harm has been done by the demand for conformity to the pre-determined picture of harm done by colonisation; facts take second place. This has serious consequences for today's social policies.

I have had direct experience with that system. By 2000 I had spent sixteen years, as a consultant for Massey University and Te Puni Kokiri, compiling a record of Maori social statistics. That research was unfettered; I was required to gather facts and I was not directed to conform to any preordained assumptions or dogma.

I then met up with the Treaty industry when I ran into trouble with the Crown Forestry Rental Trust over a demographic study of northern South Island Maori for the Victoria University Treaty of Waitangi Research Unit. By the end of the 19th century much of their land had been sold, and at the same time their population had recovered from the disastrous collapse following the inter-tribal wars of 1800-1840. The facts suggested that colonisation had done much good, and did not point to any harm linked to the sale of land. This was the wrong message for the clients; I did not find what I was employed to find, and before being paid I was directed to alter the report to imply "a disastrous impact of colonisation". I could not state any such conclusion but they were willing to pay for the resulting unclear muddle, having turned down a straightforward conclusion based on the required research.[159]

Later that same insistence of an assumed picture, even when the facts said the very opposite, came from the *New Zealand Population Review*, when a paper on Maori nineteenth century demographics was turned down because "it was essentially promoting a particular political viewpoint i.e. that European colonisation was beneficial for Maori".[160] The supposed harm of colonisation has been sustained in the public mind by the constant repetition of that mantra and the rejection of any opposing facts. Perhaps it is only those who have become involved who can fully recognise the false nature of this well-remunerated process.

The social statistics that I had gathered increasingly showed class, rather than simply ethnic, differences; I found that other social scientists were similarly coming to identify class (with the impact of recent government policies and actions) as the major cause of inequality and not ethnicity (with claims of lasting harm from long-past events). The persistence of gaps in social experiences had not been inherited from a colonial past, but were due to the policies of the day. Unfortunately, conformism to a dominant ideology directs research into a dead end; it then fails to identify problems and to determine better policies.

---

[159] Robinson 2011, pages 11 and 14; Robinson 2019, page 137
[160] Robinson 2019, page 138

Two examples of the lack of understanding of unintended consequences and the persistence with flawed policies concern the failures of family group conferences (FGC) and the support for family breakup by the domestic purposes benefit (DPB).

As a researcher I was puzzled by the general praise for the policy of family group conferences, where those leaving prison would be put in the care of their *whanau*, since studies showed extremely high rates of repeat offending (recidivism), even worse for Maori than for others. A colleague was of the opinion that the statistics were accurately telling the story, and that sending youngsters out of prison to the care of dysfunctional families did not work in practice, no matter how attractive the theory – often parents, themselves struggling with drug abuse, had to be brought from prison to the conference. I checked by phoning the programme head office in Christchurch and was told in no uncertain terms that those working at the coal face recognised the policy to be a complete disaster. But the policy was politically favoured and has continued.[161]

The domestic purposes benefit, introduced in 1973, is provided to a parent who is 19 years old or over, had a dependent child under 18, and who did not have a partner or had lost the support of their partner. In the decades of the 1980s and 1990s, high unemployment was to place additional stress on struggling families: by 1991, the unemployment rate for young Maori (for both sexes) had risen to almost 45% for those under 20, and over 30% for those 20-24 years old. Many struggling young Maori women were turning towards motherhood, which gave them the delights of children, a meaningful role and a sense of purpose in an otherwise meaningless society. The young men were mostly unemployed and lacking self-esteem, and were often violent and unwelcome – of no economic value, and thus unwanted. Those young mothers rejected the idea of a permanent

---

[161] Robinson 2019, page 61

partner and preferred to go it alone, relying on the domestic purposes benefit.

The consequences were clear: the number of Maori children under five who were living with one parent increased from around 15% in 1981 to 43% in 1991. The Maori family structure was collapsing, all too often lacking a father. The combination of unemployment and the domestic purposes benefit (worthwhile in itself) aided the destruction of the family among the large number of disadvantaged Maori. Those unintended consequences of social engineering gone wrong deserved attention. Yet in my discussions with other social researchers, I was told that to investigate this identified problem would ruin a career; there was no room for debate and progress in that world.[162]

Those who do the work understand. Those in control, who write the reports, satisfy their masters; all too often a report will present challenging facts but then will conclude with comments only supporting the status quo ideology. Thus, honest research is blocked and the decisions made are based on ignorance. I saw it then and have observed it everywhere since, more so than ever as Maori gatekeepers, with their mysterious and undefined *tikanga* and *matauranga*, can direct thinking and block independent thought.

We are in a war, the takeover of the nation by a determined group, which has been supported by the powerful Waitangi Tribunal with its separatist agenda. In the fifth century B.C., Greek dramatist Aeschylus said, "In war, truth is the first casualty". This has been repeated many times since, such as by Samuel Johnson in 1758: "among the calamities of war may be justly numbered the diminution of the love of truth, by the falsehoods which interest dictates and credulity encourages".

---

[162] Robinson 2019, page 62-64

Treaty settlements and separate Maori organisations are displacement activities, taking attention away the from modern problems of poverty and the lack of adequately paid jobs, all a consequence of globalisation, market policies and tax cuts for those better off. The benefits flow for the most part to a tribal elite.

Destruction of the Treaty of Waitangi

A search online quickly finds many sources making the revisionist claim that there were two versions of the Treaty – one in English and one in Maori, and that they are not exact translations of each other.

When writing of *Historical frictions: Maori claims and reinvented histories*, Waitangi Tribunal historian Michael Belgrave described the uncertainty. "So different are these interpretations that there can never be a 'true' meaning. ... What we call the modern treaty emerged [was invented] only in the 1970s ... This is a treaty of two texts, with major differences between them ..."[163] His chapter heading, 'Lost treaties and the making of a modern treaty', tells the story.

The 'English treaty' is written in very flowery language, in what is now known as 'Royal Style'; it is internally inconsistent and contradicts itself. This could not possibly be the result of a great deal of preparation, including lengthy instructions to Hobson and the input of those who prepared the final draft – the real treaty, which is clear, short and succinct.

This is the consequence of the continuing acceptance of the unfortunate rewrite by Hobson's secretary James Freeman, which was sent to Britain as the official copy (as explained in the earlier chapter on 'The real Treaty of Waitangi, and by Bruce Moon when describing 'Real treaty; false treaty, the true Waitangi story'[164]), and the refusal then and up to today to correct that accident of history.

The true treaty included a guarantee to all New Zealanders of "the possession of their lands, dwellings and all their property". The Freeman version extended the list, to "the full, exclusive, and undisturbed possession of their Lands and Estates, Forests, Fisheries,

---

[163] Belgrave 2005, page 45
[164] Robinson et al 2013, pages 27-51

and other properties which they may collectively or individually possess". This latter version promises the "exclusive possession of ... their fisheries", which would take away basic rights of other British subjects, the freedom of the sea, held in common.

This suggestion of two contradictory versions of the Treaty created a situation ripe for conflict. The inclusion of the word 'fisheries' in the Freeman version was ignored for a long time, until the growing Maori demands brought the question into prominence, with decisions based on the false treaty.

In 1985, the government bought back 10% of the fishing quota that it had given out and transferred that 60,000 tons to the Maori-controlled Waitangi Fisheries Commission, as well as shareholdings in fishing companies and $50 million of taxpayers' money. The giveaway was extended in the Treaty of Waitangi (Fisheries Claims) Settlement Act 1992 to include 50% of Sealord Fisheries (New Zealand's largest fishing company), 20% of all new species brought under the quota system in the future, and a further $150 million to the Waitangi Fisheries Commission. There were also special rights at a local level, *taiapure* and *mataitai* (two categories of claimed customary fishing reserves), which disadvantage the recreational fishermen of New Zealand.[165]

In the last quarter of the twentieth century the meanings of key words have been changed, and quite different versions of the Treaty were developed. In 1989, Cabinet decided to adopt a new translation by Sir Hugh Kawharu, an academic, Ngati Whatua chief, and member of the Waitangi Tribunal in 1986–1996. Here, for example, *taonga*, which Hongi Hika in 1820 had translated as 'property won at the point of the spear' (a *tao* is a spear) became 'treasures'[166] – which could mean anything and everything.

---

[165] Barr H, chapter 'Fish', Robinson et al 2013, pages249-255
[166] Belgrave et al 1989

Principles of the treaty had appeared in the 1975 Waitangi Tribunal Act, "to provide for the observance, and confirmation, of the principles of the Treaty of Waitangi ... and to determine whether certain matters are inconsistent with the principles of the Treaty".

This had little impact until 'principles' were written into law when, in 1986, Hepi Te Heuheu got Geoffrey Palmer to insert into the State-owned Enterprises Act 'Nothing in this Act shall permit the Crown to act in a manner that is inconsistent with the principles of the Treaty of Waitangi'.[167]

Since there are no principles in the Treaty, they had to be manufactured. Three of the many, and varied, versions (with 5, 10 and 11 principles) were written by The Royal Commission on Social Policy (1993), the New Zealand Maori Council (1986), and politician Doug Graham (1997).[168] A search online finds a bewildering variety of sets of principles, such as a set of 3 principles, a set of 5 principles, a partial list of 5 principles defined by a 1987 Court (as set down by a judge in the case, Justice Robin Cooke), and a 16-page article on 'Principles of the Treaty of Waitangi defined by the Waitangi Tribunal and the Court of Appeal'.[169]

Treaty Minister Doug Graham made it clear that this lack of clarity was purposeful and that Parliament had handed over the task of writing law to the courts.

"Once we talk of 'principles' of anything, it all becomes subjective and rather vague. How do we know with certainty what the principles are and in what circumstances they must be respected? Who decides what the principles are? Can Parliament decide unilaterally or should it be left to the courts, as quite independent arbiters, to declare what

---

[167] Rata 2021; Robinson 2021, pages 17-19
[168] Robinson 2011, pages 103-104
[169]
https://trc.org.nz/sites/trc.org.nz/files/digital%20library/Summary%20of%20Principles%20of%20the%20treaty_0.pdf

they are. ... Courts apply the law and, if it is unclear, interpret the law. In the 1970s and thereafter, Parliament included a reference to the Treaty of the 'principles of the Treaty' in various statutes. This was no accident or inadvertence on the part of Parliament."[170] It was an abdication of Parliament's law-making role, leaving law to be defined by unelected judges.

Then in 1987 the five justices of the Court of Appeal decided that the Treaty established a relationship 'akin to a partnership'. Such newly invented partnership is now part of official beliefs; the fifth principle in Doug Graham's list of 'principles' is that: "The Treaty signifies a relationship like a partnership based on good faith and reasonable co-operation."

With clear guidelines removed, the way has been open for wheeler-dealing, behind-the-scenes deals to give away public moneys, resources and rights. This has included retrospective top-ups to deals, such as in the settlements with Ngai Tahu and Tainui, which include a 'Relativity Mechanism' clause, which ensures that the value of their individual settlement is adjusted to the total value of all Treaty settlements. Ngai Tahu and Waikato-Tainui get a payment every 5 years to ensure the real value of their settlement remains at 16.1% and 17%, respectably, of the total. Initial relativity mechanism payments in December 2012 were $68.5 million to Ngai Tahu and $70 million to Waikato-Tainui; five-year follow-up relativity payments in December 2017 were $180 million to Ngai Tahu and $190 million to Waikato-Tainui. Such payments have nothing to do with any historical grievances.

How did that come about? "Settlement with Ngai Tahu and Tainui depended on the personal relationships between the Minister for Treaty Settlements, Douglas Graham, and the key leaders of the two tribes concerned, Tipene O'Regan and Robert Mahuta. These three knights, despite their straight talking were all committed to

---

[170] Graham 1997, page 19

negotiating settlements."[171] Thus, by such a 'gentleman's agreement', New Zealand law is decided.

Understanding of the words has been replaced by a vague prescription that destroys the very essence of good law. The Waitangi Tribunal and the courts have ruled that "the essence of the Treaty transcends the sum total of its written words and puts narrow or literal interpretation out of place. ... It is the principles of the Treaty that are to be applied, not the literal words. ... the principles that underlie the Treaty have become much more important than its precise term.[172] These Treaty principles are not set in stone; they are constantly changing as the Treaty is applied to particular issues and new situations.

The situation could not be stated more clearly. Treaty and Treaty principles are written into law – but, then, the courts state that the text is set aside, and they will judge on 'principles', a vague concept, and they refuse to tell us what they mean. **Clearly the courts can decide whatever they want.**

It is this law, combining the idea of equality set down by the pigs in *Animal Farm* ('all animals are equal, but some animals are more equal than others'), with the Maori being the privileged group (the pigs in the farm) and with the Humpty Dumpty definition of the meaning of words ('when I use a word, it means just what I choose it to mean'), that is New Zealand law. The Courts and the Waitangi Tribunal, with their absurd absence of logic, have asserted their right to define and decide law – with the accord of Parliament.

---

[171] Belgrave 2005, page 332
[172] *The Principles of the Treaty of Waitangi as expressed by the Courts and the Waitangi Tribunal*, at
https://www.waitangitribunal.govt.nz/assets/Documents/Publications/WT-Principles-of-the-Treaty-of-Waitangi-as-expressed-by-the-Courts-and-the-Waitangi-Tribunal.pdf

Activist judges have been emboldened to continue, unchecked, to invent new laws.[173] In a 2019 hearing of an appeal against the conviction of Peter Ellis, who had died the year before, Justice Joe Williams, the Supreme Court's first Maori judge, suggested that the idea that a dead person has no reputation to protect is "quite a Western idea. ... In a *tikanga* context, after death an ancestor has even more reputation to protect, is more *tapu*, has more *mana*. ... Obviously, we've got to the point where the common law has got a Maori flavour in it in *Aotearoa*."[174]

This leads to the assertion that *tikanga* is a system of law, which it is not. "The Supreme Court has just reminded us that our law is indeed sourced in two streams and that the legal profession ought to be prepared to engage with Maori law as part of the common law of New Zealand."[175] "Maori legal scholar, Ani Mikaere, has described *tikanga Maori* as 'the first law of Aotearoa' and *tikanga* has been recognised by the New Zealand state legal system in various statutes and through the common law."[176]

A judgement by Hon. Justice Powell for an order recognising customary marine title in respect of *Te Tahuna o Rangataua*, an estuary in Tauranga Harbour, similarly ruled that claims of *tikanga* override what is written in law. He believed that the Marine and Coastal Area Act 2011 (the rewrite of the previous legislation by the National government) provided a new, and different, test for customary marine title.

Then: "Williams J specifically identified *whanaungatanga* out of these core values as the glue that held the system together." Carwyn Jones had provided a similar list in his 2020 book, *Tikanga in NZ*

---

[173] Robinson 2021, pages 97-107
[174] McKenzie 2021; see also Jones 2020, Harris 2020.
[175] Jones 2020
[176] Harris 2020

common law, with five concepts, to guide the proposed separate legal system.[177]

The whole basis of law is being overturned: "there is a clear distinction in conventional *Pakeha* understandings between the body of the rules of law on the one hand and the underlying values on the other hand. *Tikanga Maori* does not draw such a clear distinction. *Tikanga Maori* includes the values themselves and does not differentiate between sanction-backed laws and advice concerning non-sanctioned customs. In *tikanga Maori*, the real challenge is to understand the values because it is these values which provide the primary guide to behaviour and not necessarily any 'rules' which may be derived from them."[178] That prescription demands a careful examination of the **behaviour** of tribes before colonisation, when *tikanga* was in force and the whole country was in mayhem.

A ruling by the High Court in 2021 made it clear that any opponent to Maori interests would be powerless against an appeal to *tikanga*: "it was not up to any court to decide whether the proposal would have an effect on Ngati He's cultural sites. That decision rested with the *hapu* and their *kaumatua* alone."[179] The determination of the meaning of the law is then with one privileged party.

The Treaty of Waitangi, with the clarity of the original, no longer exists. Also gone are the belief in equality, the refusal to countenance racial division or to condone racism, and laws that are understandable to all (including the ordinary person, the 'man on the Clapham omnibus'). New Zealanders are no longer one people.

---

[177] Jones 2016, page 66
[178] Churchman 2021 [286]
[179] Leonard 2021

A nation divided

Now we are one people
Governor Hobson at Waitangi, 1840
We are one
Prime Minister Ardern, 2019

No, Ardern is wrong, we are not now one people. New Zealanders are divided by law into two, supposedly distinct groups.

- On the one side are the Maori, defined in legislation as members of the Maori race, most if not all of mixed ancestry.
- The rest, the 'other' are also of mixed ancestry, with a similar cultural diversity, but lacking any bit of Maori blood.

This division is held to be a fundamental feature of the nation. After United Nations rapporteur Stavenhagen met and was informed by Maori groups, he wrote that: "New Zealand (*Aotearoa*) is historically a bicultural country made up basically of two ethnic components, the Maori, who trace their ancestry to the original Polynesian inhabitants, and the descendants of the European colonists and settlers, known as *Pakeha*. ... There appears to be a need for the continuation of specific measures based on ethnicity." It is as if intermarriage and living together over several generations did not happen, and unity must not be allowed.[180]

The labelling of all non-Maori as '*pakeha*' is frequent in the *He Puapua* report to government, with a proposal that a parliament for all the people should be split into a *Tikanga Maori* House for Maori

---

[180] Robinson 2021, page 50

and a *Tikanga Pakeha* House for others, overseen by a Treaty of Waitangi House for Maori and *Pakeha*.[181]

The Maori are held to have suffered grievously, leaving Maori a deprived minority in their own land (without significant improvements since 1840), as described in an invented story of wrongs of colonisation that continues today. All others are held responsible for the supposed sins of their ancestors, although most do not have ancestors from that long-ago people. Many non-Maori suffer from feelings of guilt which lead them to support modern privilege to Maori, and the 'Crown', in fact today's politicians, are willing to take moneys and rights from the people, from the common purse paid into by taxpayers, and to hand them to *iwi* leaders.

Often, reference is made to social differences, with the claim that these – mostly the consequences of the policies of and globalisation of the 1980s and 1990s – were caused by the colonisation which did so much good for Maori, bringing peace and security, demographic recovery and an increased life-span: a developed, modern way of life. But the recent period of Maori exceptionalism has seen no improvements, and payments and privileges have gone to the Maori elite and not to the struggling underclass who dominate in the oft-quoted statistics.

The differences have mushroomed over the past fifty years, with a considerable acceleration of division. New Zealand is now deeply, fundamentally, a nation of two peoples.

There is separated **voting registration**, separate **seats in parliament** and **wards in local bodies**, a separate **political party**.

Mention has been made previously of a 46-page list of **treaty payments** and a 12-page list of 98 **acts of parliament** giving special rights for Maori.

---

[181] Robinson 2021, page 74

Many wealthy Maori companies (as in Tainui and Ngai Tahu) are registered as charities and are **exempt from paying income tax.**

Exemption of rates for Maori freehold land may be allowed by a local authority.

Government agencies need to ensure that **at least 5% of the number of relevant contracts** awarded are to Maori businesses

As noted above, changes in law, including recognition of *tikanga*, provide **additional legal rights** to Maori.[182]

As also noted above, **fishing quota, a fishing company and customary fishing rights** have been assigned to Maori.

A government proposal is to hand **the infrastructure and control of fresh water systems** to a national structure with Maori having half the part in the choice of directors and an effective veto.[183]

The Department of Conservation 'Options Development Group', with eight members nominated by *whanau, hapu, iwi* and Maori organisations, has made a recommendation that **conservation land is governed by a partnership** between *tangata whenua* and the department, guided by *matauranga Maori*.[184] One recent *hui* has recommended the transfer of the ownership and control of the entire conservation estate to tribal authorities.[185]

There is a **separate curriculum** for Maori schools.

---

[182] Robinson 2021, pages 97-108
[183] Robinson 2021, pages 134-139
[184] https://www.doc.govt.nz/globalassets/documents/our-work/options-development-group/options-development-group-report-march-2022.pdf
[185] https://www.scoop.co.nz/stories/PA2105/S00075/govt-must-be-upfront-about-its-plans-for-doc-land.htm

The **national school curriculum is being rewritten to emphasise** *matauranga* **with a focus on colonisation** rather than the full story of the nation.[186]

A separate **Maori Health Authority** has been set up, to work with *Iwi*-Maori Partnership Boards, Maori health providers, *iwi*, *hapu* and Maori communities to "understand Maori health needs" across New Zealand.[187]

Government **funding of $105 million to the media requires adherence to a Maori viewpoint**, with commitments to the reformulated Treaty, to Maori as 'a *Te Tiriti* partner' (insisting on the false idea of a 'partnership') and to '*te reo Maori*'.[188]

The formation of separate Maori units within government departments, giving directions to all staff regarding the requirements of *tikanga* and *matauranga*, provide employment for a cadre of gatekeepers, resulting in increased Maori control over all elements of government.

The reach of Maori activists to govern separately has even spread to international affairs; a national conference on Maori perspectives on the great international issues of our time was organised at Te Papa in July, 2022.[189]

That list was for the most part put together last year (2021). There will be more. Some of the further divisions planned for New Zealand are considered in later chapters, such as that on co-governance.

---

[186] Roger Childs on Waikanae Watch
https://waikanaewatch.org/2021/04/23/getting-a-balanced-history-curriculum/;
Robin son 2021, pages 118-127
[187] Robinson 2021, pages 128-133
[188] Robinson 2021, page 8
[189] https://www.diplosphere.org/conference

Rewriting history and redefinition of racism

Who controls the past controls the future: who controls the present controls the past.
George Orwell in *Nineteen Eighty-Four*, 1949

Give me a child until he is seven and I will show you the man.
Aristotle, often attributed to Francis Xavier and Ignatius of Loyola

These well-known sayings reflect the importance of the assertion of a chosen view of the past, of upbringing and education in forming each person. This is obvious, as young people are told of the world into which they have been born.

Many of today's vocal Maori belong to the first generation of *Kohanga Reo* and *Kaupapa Maori* pupils, who have been given a separate and very different education, paid for and supported by the state, with very different values, ideals and beliefs. Such racial separation will continue throughout their lives, with *hui* (often organised for them by Government) to define government policy for all New Zealanders – a disturbing exercise of social engineering whereby this somewhat isolated group develops and conserves a set of beliefs totally alien to those of the remainder of society.

The result is an ideology that calls for the transformation of the national way of life, supporting a revolutionary overthrow of the modern system of government. Separate education, privileges and rights have nurtured an alien ideology.

This is wrong; the focus on the past should firstly be on the building of a nation and the advances brought by colonisation, with a settled national government and a system of law. If we are to consider past wrongs and breaking of the Treaty, then at the top of the list – by far – must be the armed rebellions, with the breaking of the law, setting up of a separate kingite monarchy, murder of other New Zealanders by armed groups, and illegal occupation of settlers' and government land. Those facts have been hidden, and lies have been repeated to obscure and hide the reality. Instead, there has been an emphasis on harm done to those rebels, with claims of past wrongdoing.

Often these accounts have been fanciful or simply untrue. Claims of the burning of a church full of women and children at Rangiaowhia have been repeated time and again; Bruce Moon lists seven examples.[190] In fact, there were two churches at Rangiaowhia, both of which were standing at the end of the skirmish in 1864; the Anglican church is still standing and the Catholic church was demolished in 1931.

Otorohanga secondary school students on Moon's list were clearly distressed at what they had been led to believe. "We were shocked and horrified by the stories told by the *kaumatua*, who were distraught sharing their ancestors' stories about innocent women and children and elders being burned alive", said one of these students.[191] Bruce Moon later wrote to the principals of eight colleges (Fairfield College, Fraser High School, Sacred Heart, St Paul's Collegiate, Waikato Diocesan School for Girls, Rotorua Girls' High School and Hamilton Girls' High School) whose students had listened to that presentation to ask them to ensure that the truth is paramount in what students are taught, but received no response. Piers Seed, in a thorough and comprehensive description of all aspects of those events, based on eye-witness accounts, has shown that this did not happen – it is all fabricated.[192]

A similar, painstaking report of Parihaka, again based on all the written accounts of the time, does not make reference to frequently

---

[190] Moon 2018
[191] Seed 2022, page 121
[192] Seed 2022

repeated modern myths of great harm; those claims only appeared much later, built up well after the event.[193]

There is much extreme language in official reports as well as in the media. Thus: "The graphic *muru* of most of Taranaki and the *raupatu* without ending describe the **holocaust** of Taranaki history and the denigration of the founding peoples in a continuum from 1840 to the present."

Continuing the quote: "This sentence of the Waitangi Tribunal's first Taranaki report, which caused much controversy because of its perceived overstatement, follows a summary in the final chapter which veritably shakes with anger. The tribunal concludes that 'the whole history of Government dealings with Maori in Taranaki has been the antithesis to that envisaged by the Treaty of Waitangi. ... The invasion and sacking of Parihaka, 'must rank with the most heinous action of any government, in any country, in the last century.'"[194]

This was widely criticised, and Associate Maori Affairs Minister Tariana Turia was forced to apologise for repeating those sentiments, for offending anyone over her comparison of Maori colonisation to the Holocaust. Of course, the damage was done; the one-sided and extreme depiction of New Zealand history has created anger by spreading myths and ignoring the true story of killings (of Maori by Maori) in Taranaki Maori feuds, of why war began and what actually took place.

Such myths have become widely accepted. For example, a secondary school history teacher from the southern Waikato e-mailed Tross Publishing to say that the statement in the book, 'One Law or Two Monarchs'[195] that no church was burned down at Rangiaowhia was wrong. Tross Publishing e-mailed back stating that both churches

---

[193] McLean 2020
[194] Bennion 1996
[195] Robinson and Childs 2018

were still standing after the engagement there between colonial troops and the Kingite rebels in the incident of 1864 and that one of the two churches is still standing while the other was demolished in 1931. To this clear statement of a fact the teacher replied "**That is only your perspective**". But surely, history is about facts and not perspective – either the churches were burned down or they weren't and in this case they weren't. It is alarming to think that gullible secondary school students are being taught by biased history teachers who cannot even identify a historical fact based on clear evidence if it gets in the way of their own prejudices.

The schoolteacher's rejection of facts does, however, receive support from the Waitangi Tribunal in their acceptance of 'reinvented histories'. "Historical narratives developed ... New ways emerged of describing what had occurred ... Not only did these reinvented histories have to be fashioned for presentation to commissions of inquiry and courts, they also had to become part of the dialogue between the government and Maori communities over later policies. ... The kinds of historical narrative that emerged were not, therefore, simply eye-witness accounts remembered by participants and handed down to a new generation. The narratives were discussed on *marae*, where they were challenged and polished, prepared by witnesses at commissions of inquiry, and then transformed into legal judgements and commission reports."[196] Thus is history rewritten to suit a legal challenge, with a significant reward awaiting the claimants. And we are all expected to believe such nonsense.

The fundamental rewriting of history, to bring the narrative of the past into line with the current dominant ideology, is well recognised, and has become known as 'revisionism', 'presentism' and 'counterfactual' history.[197]

---

[196] Belgrave 2005, pages 25-28
[197] Robinson 2012, pages 238-242

Historian Bill Oliver has written of an elusive way of writing and using history, which is then a type of history created in an atmosphere clouded with retrospective recrimination and that the Tribunal has, along with the law courts, become an important 'voice' of the Treaty in recent years, reinterpreting the Treaty and Treaty principles in the light of present concerns.[198] Thus, "the reports exemplify an instrumental but – because never explicitly avowed – elusive way of writing and using history [with] a historical mentality less concerned to recapture past reality than to embody present aspiration. [There is] an instrumental presentism which is remarkably evidence-free ... shaped by a current political agenda."[199]

In that way the Tribunal has generated "a 'counterfactual' history of policies and institutions" and the construction of a "retrospective utopia" based on "a Maori view of history". This is counterfeit history, a fake, as: "The adversary courtroom leads parties to seek and interpret the past to support or deny present claims, not to find what really happened in all its complexity."[200]

Historian Michael Belgrave has recognised many aspects of this process, which were evident in his time as researcher and research manager for the Waitangi Tribunal. "Historians have questioned the Tribunal's reports, accusing them of failing to abide by the rules of academic history in suggesting that the Crown could have acted differently in the past, according to rules established in the present. ... Historians have recognised that the kind of history produced by a commission of inquiry is different from academic history. ... a commission of inquiry writes history within a distinct cultural tradition ... In New Zealand this form of history has been called *hapu* history or *kaupapa Maori* (Maori-centred) history. It attempts to

---

[198] Byrnes 2004, pages 2 and 152
[199] Oliver W H. *The future behind us, the Waitangi Tribunal's retrospective utopia.* In Sharp and McHugh 2001
[200] Sharp A. *Recent juridical and constitutional histories of Maori.* In Sharp and McHugh 2001

break with the Western tradition of interpreting the past, relying not only on a Maori-centred view of history, but on a view of history that reflects the perspective [here that word again, perspective, allowing separate realities] of specific communities. The emphasis is on *whakapapa* (genealogy), oral tradition and *whare wananga* (centres of learning) by which a community's understanding of its past is transferred and updated from one generation to the next. ... The polarisation of opinion in Muriwhenua shows the extent to which professional historical evidence could become driven by the adversarial nature of a legal inquiry. ... Oliver was particularly critical of the way in which the tribunal had created a utopian counter-factual past that could never have existed in colonial New Zealand."[201]

Tribal myths, together with behind-the-scene dealings between lawyers, politicians and tribal leaders, should not define history and thus influence, and determine, current policies and actions. History should report what actually happened, based on facts – the eye-witness evidence that is set aside by Waitangi Tribunal.

The resulting imaginary picture, ignoring any failings of Maori and damning the British for not acting in an impossible way – to suit one particular modern ideology – has, as intended, created a guilt trap, so that many New Zealanders came to wish to atone for the claimed (and often manufactured) wrongs of the past. This has led to a belief that Maori must be given enormous recompense for the supposed wrongs of some of our ancestors against Maori, along with special rights that destroy the foundations of our democracy.

This is racism, directing the affairs of a nation. It has destroyed any sense of common citizenship, of a united nation, or that we are one. A deep belief in equality and an understanding of civic or political ideals, fundamental to the underlying ethics of our civilisation and what makes a modern developed society, is gone. We no longer share

---

[201] Belgrave 2005, pages 2, 35,123, 282

a pride in being New Zealanders, rather being asked to assume the shame of past wrongdoing.

That has set the scene for a new, opposite, operational definition of racism. True racism is a belief in race, and giving different treatments to groups of peoples based on race. **This has been turned on its head; now those who argue for equality and against racism are labelled and attacked as 'racists'. We live, in so many ways, through the looking glass.**

The end of freedom of speech

People die, but books never die. No man and no force can take from the world the books that embody man's eternal fight against tyranny.
Franklin D. Roosevelt, a Message to the Booksellers of America, 6 May, 1942.

Recognition of the importance of books, and free speech, has long been part of our civilisation. John Stuart Mill, an English philosopher, political economist, Member of Parliament and civil servant, (one of the most influential thinkers in the history of classical liberalism, who contributed widely to social theory, political theory, and political economy) set down the case against censorship in 1869, reflecting British beliefs at the time of New Zealand colonisation.

"Let us suppose, therefore, that the government is entirely at one with the people, and never thinks of exerting any power of coercion unless in agreement with what it conceives to be their voice. But I deny the right of the people to exercise such coercion, either by themselves or by their government. The power itself is illegitimate. The best government has no more title to it than the worst. It is as noxious, or more noxious, when exerted in accordance with public opinion, than when in opposition to it. If all mankind minus one, were of one opinion, and only one person were of the contrary opinion, mankind would be no more justified in silencing that one person, than he, if he had the power, would be justified in silencing mankind. ... the peculiar evil of silencing the expression of an opinion is that it is robbing the human race; posterity as well as the existing generation; those who dissent from the opinion, still more than those who hold it. If the opinion is right, they are deprived of the opportunity of exchanging error for truth: if wrong, they lose, what is almost as great a benefit, the clearer perception and livelier impression of truth, produced by its collision with error."[202]

The dangers of denial of free speech, and of publication of opinion unacceptable to a government or its agencies, was most dramatically shown in the Nazi burning of 25,000 'un-German' books in Berlin's Opera Square on May 10, 1933, following a fiery address by Joseph Goebbels ('No to decadence and moral corruption!'), and the events which followed.

We once had this precious heritage, a belief in free speech, as part of our culture, but now Television New Zealand would have us ban books that they do not approve of – including this one that you are reading now. On Saturday 4 December and Sunday 12 December, 2021, TV1 News broadcast an appeal to bookstores and libraries to refuse to stock books by Tross Publishing – a call to ban those books. I was referred to explicitly, and one programme was illustrated by the covers of two of my books, *The corruption of New Zealand democracy; a Treaty overview* (2011) and *He Puapua: Blueprint for breaking up New Zealand* (2021). The two broadcasts, which are available online, were headed "Educators say publishers' books **anti-Maori, hateful and untrue**"[203] and "Company accused of anti-Maori publishing promoting books at schools".[204] Tross has been publishing since 2010; it was evident that the incentive for these attacks was anger with my recent book explaining the *He Pupua* report, and my strong condemnation of the separatist agenda.

Those claims were not backed by any facts; they are nonsense. The points in my books most critical of Maori ways referred to the turmoil, killing and social disruption of the early nineteenth century tribal wars. That description is simply true, and indicates a concern

---

[202] Mill 1869
[203] https://www.1news.co.nz/2021/12/04/educators-say-publishers-books-anti-maori-hateful-and-untrue/
[204] https://www.1news.co.nz/2021/12/12/company-accused-of-anti-maori-publishing-promoting-books-at-schools/

for Maori well-being, and a celebration that colonisation brought an end to that widespread fighting. As for being 'anti-Maori', if they had read my books they would have noted *Two great New Zealanders, Tamati Waka Nene and Apirana Ngata* (2015), which tells of a great respect for these early Maori leaders; to this one can add the appreciation of Te Wherowhero, up to his death in 1860, and for Rewi Maniapoto when the kingite war had ended. These were very real human beings, whose thoughts can be followed today by reference to written reports of their conversations and their actions. Those broadcasts were themselves hateful and untrue.

The reporter, Te Aniwa Hurihanganui, had first contacted Tross Publishing asking for my email address. Our reply was that this would be provided if the reporting was fair and accurate: "Dr Robinson would be prepared to discuss this important issue openly so long as he be accorded fair treatment by your media outlet."

Her intention was made clear in the response, refusing that condition; there would be no fair treatment: "I'd like to interview or get a written response from a representative of Tross Publishing – rather than Dr Robinson as originally requested." She then describes her true intention: "we're planning to run a story alleging that the books published by Tross Publications are described as untrue, false, hateful, disgusting, and anti-Maori." The issue was pre-judged and the programme content was planned prior to any interview. Their aim was to prevent conversation between people with differing views, to try to ban our books, to stifle debate, and to strengthen the call for division of our nation.[205]

---

[205] See articles *TV1 News has proposed a ban on sales of books*, Waikanae Watch https://waikanaewatch.org/2021/12/10/tv1-news-wants-books-it-doesnt-like-banned/ and *the hit job by TV1 News on Tross Publishing is a hit job on freedom of speech*, Waikanae Watch https://waikanaewatch.org/2021/12/17/the-hit-job-by-tv1-news-on-tross-publishing-is-a-hit-job-on-freedom-of-speech/, and the video *Fake TV One News Try to Ban Books* https://www.youtube.com/watch?v=2kkumkgvCQM, which can be watched on

Strident views were presented, as if they were well-founded, behind a cloak of quotes, none of which gave any factual basis for the opinion expressed. The important issues supposedly at stake were never covered, and there was no clear point which demanded rebuttal.

An English literature tutor, Brittany Rose, reacted sharply when shown a row of books: "I looked closer and it was disgusting. ... It just struck me as incredibly insensitive, ill-informed and damaging." She did not like the books, fine, but made no specific criticisms.

University of Auckland Senior Maori studies lecturer, Dr Daniel Hikuroa, was equally 'disgusted'. "*He Puapua* is a document that's designed to give life to the treaty. And these materials that are coming out... they call on half-truths and out-right lies. It's the out-right lies that I find really dangerous." I am the author of the book on *He Puapua* displayed in the programme, but this is empty posturing; I am called a liar, with no facts requiring rebuttal. If there are lies in the book, he must state them clearly; he did not.

There was no content to the programmes, no factual criticisms of these books pointing to supposedly incorrect information, just proclamations of grievance without explanation or proof. That crude attack shocked many people and several complaints were made; all were dismissed without serious consideration.

TVNZ Head of News and Current Affairs Paul Yurisich thought that quoting statements without any concern for their veracity was fine: "Our journalist Te Aniwa Hurihanganui was not, as you state 'using her privileged position as a journalist to undertake political activism' but rather reporting on and delving into issues raised by others. I am confident in the editing process we have in place." But the editing process never considered fact-checking of the outrageous claims.[206]

---

television: go to YouTube and search for 'Andy Oakley' where it is included in a list of videos.
[206] Private communication, Susan Short

Following two complaints, the TVNZ Complaints Committee decided that there had been no breach of standards: "The Committee finds that Tross Publishing and Dr Robinson were treated fairly in the broadcast."[207] This is nonsense. My reply was a demand to join in a fair debate; my desire was, and is, for open debate, to explain and clarify points of contention. Nothing is gained from hurling abuse, by a crude attack with no desire for meeting, never listening to one another with an open – and polite – exchange of views organised by a professional and unbiased organisation.

They discussed some of the supposed standards which guide them. "The purpose of this Standard [9, accuracy] is to protect the public from being significantly misinformed. The audience may be misinformed in two ways: by incorrect statements of fact within the program and/or by being misled by the program. Where statements of fact are at issue, the standard is concerned only with material inaccuracy. Technical or unimportant points unlikely to significantly affect the audience's understanding of the program as a whole are not material. Being 'misled' is defined as being 'given a wrong idea or impression of the facts'.

It was entirely accurate to state that the Tross Publishing books referred to in the story have been described as 'anti-Maori, hateful and untrue' [they found someone to say this] and 'insensitive, ill-informed and damaging'. Those were descriptions used by people interviewed in the programme. You have not made any allegation that a material point of fact was inaccurate in the programme." [I myself could find no material point of fact in the programme, which could be corrected; it is all a series of slurs and insults.]

This is blatant trickery by journalists who are practised at being economical with the truth and getting out dodgy, sensational complaints. They know how to attack, to ignore the facts by just quoting someone, no matter how extreme and absurd the claims.

---

[207] Private communication, Peter Martel

For them the requirement for balance and 'a range of other perspectives' was satisfied by the second programme which followed the format of the first and repeated the unfounded charges. Their statement is ludicrous: "On 12 December 1 News broadcast a follow-up to this story, which expanded on the issue discussed in this program and provided further perspectives." To say the same thing twice is neither balance nor another perspective.

The Broadcasting Minister, Kris Faafoi, did not reply to a letter from Tross Publishing. I myself thought that *The Listener* should explore the issues raised by this savage attack on free speech and sent a short article. The reply from the Editor was polite but dismissive: "I completely understand your concern over your treatment by TVNZ, but this is an issue you need to take up with either them, or the Broadcasting Standards Authority, which has an official complaints process." It is difficult to fight against the lack of expressed concern at such an attack, and the general media refusal to provide fair coverage of the overturn of New Zealand freedom of speech and democracy.

This was followed, on 25 July, 2022, by another attack, on Piers Seed's book *Hoani's Last Stand*, with similar claims: "That this book is harmful, upsetting, biased and makes a lie of the oral accounts passed down by *tupuna*", and that "this book should be taken off shelves and read with caution". The publisher responded with a simple statement: "Tross Publishing rejects every one of these allegations as the book is based on all the known written eye-witness accounts of the time – both native and European – which are given in full at the end, and not on oral accounts that can be unreliable – especially after several generations."

The action referred to here, the taking of the 'breadbasket', Rangiaowhia, near Te Awamutu, towards the end of the king movement wars of rebellion, was arguably the most sensible decision made by any British commander. The march around three recently constructed, well-fortified hill-top *pa* removed the need to surround and bombard (and perhaps storm) those strongholds and undoubtedly saved many lives, among both Maori rebels and British troops.

The incident involved an attempt by the British to move people away from one *whare* (which was in fact a solid building made of heavy wooden slabs; almost half the area was dug out to a depth of three feet, similar to a purpose-built rifle pit). Fighting began when Sergeant McHale was shot by an armed warrior inside the *whare*, as was Colonel Nixon when coming to his aid (both died). Some women and children who agreed to leave moved away to safety; the men could have joined them but decided to stay and fight. A firefight followed, which ended with the burning of the *whare*; ten Maori died there.[208]

It is well known that both of the two churches in the village were standing after the fighting; this was not challenged in the TVNZ item. There is, however, in the news item an imaginative, unidentified video of a *whare* with a cross above the door being attacked, as if it had been used as a church – which is nowhere found in any eye-witness account.

Two Maori voiced complaints based on tribal story-telling. 'Historian' Vincent O'Malley very carefully said effectively nothing: "There are multiple eye-witness accounts that that indicate that this happened." He provided no clarity despite having written about the incident in his book, *The New Zealand wars*[209] – where he had ignored eye-witness accounts and failed to mention that the fight at the fatal *whare* started when an armed Maori inside shot and killed Sergeant McHale who was asking that they move out and away. There is a desperate need in the mainstream media for scholarship to at least a rudimentary standard, so clearly absent in these several attacks by TV1 News.

---

[208] Seed 2022, pages 71-76
[209] O'Malley 2019, pages 121-124

There have been many such attacks, leading many to duck for cover, to withdraw from the debate; thinking for yourself and holding a contrary view is dangerous. Don Brash is the most well-known spokesman for equality, and he has been attacked frequently. But he is by no means alone; the attacks have been widespread, on anyone speaking out for equality and daring to warn of the serious consequences of separatism, which is threatening the destruction of foundations of society: truth, democracy and freedom of information. Rudeness and the refusal to listen to, or allow, other than what is sanctioned, is common. I hear of similar happenings frequently, but I do not have to look far for examples; there are enough from my own experiences – such as the above, and the following.

In 2021, I sent a letter to the *Northland Age*, raising a concern about the frequent label of racism put on those who call for equality. The Editor, Peter Jackson, replied promptly that he would publish it, but a day later he phoned to tell me that the article would no longer be published, as he had been instructed to forward any such material higher up the organisation's chain of control for vetting, establishing a censorship system that removed the choice from the Editor to the paper's owner, NZME (New Zealand Herald), thus destroying any semblance of editorial independence and freedom of the press.[210]

Open discussion of history is often blocked. The Otaki Historical Society told me that I was too 'controversial'. Once I turned up to talk to a Petone group to find an empty unlit hall – the committee changed their mind and decided that I was not cosher so they cancelled without telling me. On the other hand, I have given a number of talks such as to the Kapiti Historical Society and to the University of the Third Age, which were well attended and concluded in lively question sessions.

Retired physicist and avid historian Bruce Moon faced similar problems in 2018 when he was invited by the Nelson Institute to give

---

[210] Robinson 2021, page 94

a talk on New Zealand's 'fake history', related to Treaty of Waitangi issues. Shortly before the scheduled talk it was cancelled, called off due to 'health and safety' concerns, which Moon interpreted as threats of violence. Two months later, a venue was found; the room was packed, and the presentation well received.[211]

That year, Don Brash was barred from speaking at Massey University when the vice-chancellor, Jan Thomas, decided to stop the event because of heightened tensions over free speech in New Zealand. Then, as a speaker at the University of Auckland's Debating Society in a debate over freedom of speech (Brash was for freedom of speech), he was heckled and prevented from speaking.[212] Brash received further ill-mannered treatment in 2021 when speaking against separate Maori wards at a Tauranga meeting.[213]

You might imagine that there would be some protection against that abuse, and support for the right of free speech, perhaps from the supposed gatekeeper of citizens' rights, the Human Rights Commission. Their Race Relations Office claims to stands for "social inclusion: We all have the right to be treated fairly, with respect and to be free from unwelcome racial discrimination." But the very opposite proved to be the case.[214]

In 2013 Hugh Barr and I took our concern to the Commission that many speaking for equality were being labelled as 'racist'.

---

[211] https://www.democracyaction.org.nz/free_speech_bruce_moon_speaks_out_in_nelson
[212] https://www.newshub.co.nz/home/new-zealand/2018/08/we-stand-against-what-he-represents-don-brash-heckled-at-auckland-university-speaking-event.html
[213] https://www.nzherald.co.nz/bay-of-plenty-times/news/war-of-words-tauranga-residents-butt-heads-at-controversial-maori-ward-meeting/5QAPDKYPSD7DWRVSFDQM7KR3UA/
[214] Robinson 2021, pages 147-148

Although we had been told that: "Our preferred method of discussion about these issues is through 'dialogue' which has a focus on listening to each other's view in order to 'strengthen relationships'", we were treated rudely and the meeting was confrontational and adversarial.[215]

Our conclusion was that the Race Relations Commission is an indoctrination agency promoting *iwi* rights over the rights of other New Zealanders. Their view appeared to be based on three beliefs: untold wrongs were committed against *iwi* by the British Colonial Governors and the settler governments, and restoration is essential through the Treaty Claim process; thousands of Maori were killed by the settler armies during land wars between 1840 and the 1860s; the 'partnership' principle demands that *iwi* have a direct share in governance, and have co-management. The Race Relations Commission is like a religious sect, and these tenets are sacred and true to them. There is no comprehension of universal human rights; they were too caught up in the ideology of exceptionalism.

We met a closed mindset; there was no dialogue. They refused to consider the issue that we were attempting to raise, that many who were speaking for equality, against racism, were called 'racist'. In their minds different rights must be accepted and so racism is now, here in New Zealand, the very opposite to the dictionary definition.

That thinking is uncomfortably similar to the words of the twentieth century's major imagined dystopias (unhappy futures, the opposite of utopias). Here the claims of the pigs in Orwell's *Animal Farm* are voiced by Maori claimants for a special position in co-governance: "All animals are equal but some animals are more equal". The insistence to follow an official line imitates the directions of Huxley's *Brave New World*: "One believes things because one has been conditioned to believe them. Great is truth, but still greater, from a practical point of view, is silence about truth."

---

[215] Barr and Robinson 2013

To speak this truth, to identify this racism, is damaging to career and position. In today's New Zealand, freedom of speech is available only to those with nothing to lose, such as those with no position or career to protect, mostly towards the end of our lives. I am retired and fit those requirements, while others must keep their heads down.

Going backwards. Guests at the Lake House, Lake Waikaremoana, when the area was a national park available to all New Zealanders. However, in order to buy the votes of the race-based Maori Party in Parliament, the National Government of John Key handed over the whole of this Urewera National Park to the small, private Tuhoe tribe which, as the photo below shows, did not waste time in declaring their hostility towards the people of New Zealand.

A Snake in the Garden!

Promotional material from an alternative government, verging on treason.

MAORI GOVERNMENT OF AOTEAROA NU TIRENI

Te Wakaminenga Maori Government of Aotearoa Nu Tireni

The de jure Government of the Chiefs of the Confederation of the United Tribes - Nga Rangatira o Nga Hapu o Nu Tireni

WARNING TRESPASS NOTICE!

TO ALL NEW ZEALAND GOVERNMENT OR LOCAL COUNCIL REPRESENTATIVES, POLICE, MILITARY OR OFFICERS OF Her Majesty the Queen in Right of New Zealand or Corporate representatives

YOU MAY NOT ENTER WITHOUT CONSENT

The Occupants within this property including the land itself, are under the protection and authority of the United Tribes of New Zealand as laid out in the lawful document, He Wakaputanga 1835 / The Declaration of Independence 1835 specifically in; Article 1,clauses a,b,c & d, Article 2, clauses a,b,c,d & e, Article 3, clauses a & b and Article 4, clauses f,g,h,i and j.

The flag herein this notice, and that is situated on this Private Land, affirms this property and it's occupants are under the jurisdictional authority and protection of Nga Rangatira o Nga Hapu o Te Wakaminenga o Nu Tireni, Aotearoa (Congress of Māori Chiefs) who act under the authority of He Wakaputanga 1835 also known as the Declaration of Independence 1835. Failure to understand or recognise what this means is not an excuse to breach this authority.

Trespass is an OFFENCE. You may not enter this property under any pretense, order or reason unless approved by the Head of the House. Violation of this notice will be subject to & judged by a Paa Kooti, a Marae based court and subject to murutanga – compensation & justice as administered by the duly authorised Rangatira who shall preside, determine, prosecute and execute punishment according to Ture Tikanga, Māori customary law.

The occupants here on this land are protected under He Wakaputanga 1835 and Common Law jurisdiction and have not entered into or agreed to a contract of engagement with the New Zealand Government also known as 'Her Majesty the Queen in Right of New Zealand' or any other Council or Corporate entity.

TRESPASS DAMAGES shall apply if YOU step onto this Private Property. Minimum Penalty – NZD $10,000.00 (Ten Thousand New Zealand Dollars)

Per Person, Per Entry. This Penalty is at the discretion of the occupiers and is the basis of claim to be considered by the Paa Kooti in consideration of the breach. By your Trespass you agree to provide full details of your private information to the House Holder.

YOU HAVE BEEN GIVEN FAIR NOTICE!
(By Order Of The House Holder Under He Wakaputanga 1835 & Common Law authority.)

Isaac Newton, who developed "Newtonian mechanics". For 25 years he was President of the Royal Society in London. The background is his college at Cambridge, Trinity, which had also produced Francis Bacon (below), who promoted inductive reasoning in scientific investigation. Here the setting is Gray's Inn, one of the Inns of Court in London, where Bacon lived and studied. New Zealand has benefited enormously from science which, being universal, cannot be compared with "tikanga" and "matauranga Maori" as the Royal Society of New Zealand has so foolishly suggested.

A ruthless ideology

I may disagree with what you have to say, but I shall defend, to the death, your right to say it.
attributed to Voltaire

Let a hundred flowers bloom; let a hundred schools of thought contend.
Mao Tse Tung, May 1956

Mao had used his speech to signal what he had wanted from the intellectuals of the country, for different and competing ideologies to voice their opinions about the issues of the day. He wanted China to escape from the rigidity of his own vision of communism, where all were living in communes. Sadly, Mao later became fearful of the reassertion of a bourgeois way of life and, in 1966, he launched the Cultural Revolution, when many suffered from the excesses of the fanatical Red Guards. China has, since, taken the path of a mixed economy, and has flourished. There are many examples throughout history of the dangers of closed thinking (Nazism and its burning of books is mentioned above), contrasting with the prosperity of an open society.

A common view, and shared values and beliefs (a 'paradigm'), is an essential glue to hold together communities and a national society. "A 'frame' is a social theory that holds that people have, through their lifetimes, built a series of mental emotional filters, which they use to make sense of the world. Frames, as emotional filters, influence the choices we make. ... This gives the sender and framer of the information enormous power to use these schemas to influence how the receivers will interpret the message."[216]

While such an overarching, common worldview brings people together, individuals and groups will have their own particular cultural beliefs (Christian, Islam, atheist, etc.) which coexist within the national framework (including acceptance of law) in a pluralistic society.

Problems with dysfunctional ideas are constantly faced in any civilisation – such as the expansion of terrorist groups across the world in recent years. A more serious problem arises when some individual group gains dominance and behaves like a fundamentalist sect, to become dictatorial and insist that all must owe allegiance to their particular ideology and follow their dictates. When such extremism takes over a nation, the situation becomes dangerous (as Nazism in Germany, cultural revolution in China).

The British brought with them the beliefs of the eighteenth-century Age of Enlightenment: that we all belong to one common humanity, not separated by race; that all are equal; that – within the law – people should be left to worship as they please, and to hold to diverse cultural views. That plurality was on display at Rangiaowhia, where two churches, Catholic and Anglican, co-existed in a Maori village.

There was no imposition of an introduced culture on Maori other than the acceptance of a national government, and peace with an end to tribal warfare and cannibalism.[217] The great cultural transformation of the nineteenth century was carried out by Maori themselves.[218] It was Maori who chose Christianity over their traditional beliefs and chose to take many positive actions, such as the setting free of slaves (before and after 1840, and before any firm action by the new colonial

---

[216] Butler 2014
[217] Robinson 2016, pages 25-33
[218] Robinson 2012, pages 87-92; Robinson 2016, pages 20-25; Robinson 2020, pages 108-111

regime).[219] Maori were given opportunities; if some among the chiefs, such as Tamihana Te Rauparaha, lived as English gentlemen, it was their choice. It was left to Maori to protect what they valued; the task of government was to allow the freedom to choose for themselves.

While living, and prospering, within the new nation, many did wish to hold on to many aspects of their traditional culture, *tikanga*, such as Apirana Ngata: "Throughout his life, both in Parliament and after, Ngata focussed much of his attention on the revitalisation of the Maori culture that had long been a pleasure to him".[220] Ngata spoke in 1929 of the importance of the preservation of the Maori language but in 1936 he insisted on the use of English alone in schools, before changing his mind in 1939. The story of the formal use of Maori is not simple; much of the pressure to use English alone had come from Maori chiefs.

It was a non-Maori scholar, Richard Benton (leader of a study of the use of the Maori language in a series of interviews in 1973 and 1979) who raised the alarm, showing that Maori use was in rapid decline and in danger of disappearing.[221] This led to a considerable effort – by government – to revitalise *te reo*. When a call was made for help, it was answered.

Over recent decades, New Zealand has seen the growing presence of a way of thinking that shuts out open debate and demands subservience to a narrow orthodoxy. This comes from an increasingly separated section of the population who develop, exchange and propagate a perception of the world with a closed mindset, a form of groupthink, a narrow ideology which drives towards a distorted account of history.[222]

---

[219] Robinson 2022
[220] Robinson 2015, pages 265-281
[221] Benton 1997
[222] Robinson 2019, pages 31-38; Robinson 2021, pages 144-146

Maori meetings at *hui* are a regular feature of life on or around a *marae*. There is an interchange of ideas, and a common view is formed. A problem arises when the issues and ideas considered there are not shared with others, since a particular worldview develops in that separated group that needs to be challenged and questioned, adapted or rejected, to fit the requirements of the whole community.

Many such *hui* deal with Waitangi Tribunal hearings and Treaty of Waitangi settlements, often supported and funded by government. The aim is to further Maori interests, to put forward grievances and grounds for recompense, to build a narrative of past wrongs and to gain increased payments from the state.

The expansion of grounds for grievance has resulted in the resuscitation and spreading of myths developed during past conflicts – stories built up after an event, often with no eye-witness account – 'confirmation bias', to "favour and recall information in a way that confirms or supports one's prior beliefs and values", providing propaganda for a one-sided picture of events. Invented tales of what happened at Rangiaowhia and Parihaka are two such examples.[223] This process has been supported by the Waitangi Tribunal, which accepts and places great importance on 'oral history'.

The outcome is no surprise. Too many Maori have formed a particular view of the world (referred to above as their worldview, frame of reference, paradigm); they have come to see themselves as an aggrieved first people who deserve special position and entitlement, and an independent role in governance, separate from that of all other New Zealanders – a dangerous ideology, with no belief in equality and a dismissal of democracy.

The claim is that the determining factor, when deciding the worth of a person and the place in their scheme, is ancestry. Those with just a drop of Maori blood (and most, if not all, are of mixed race) are special. They deny the call of great fighters against racism, such as

---

[223] Seed 2022, page 85

Martin Luther King in the USA, with his dream of an end to racism: "I have a dream that my four little children will one day live in a nation where they will not be judged by the colour of their skin but by the content of their character."

We, in New Zealand, are to be judged by 'the colour of our skin', be it ever so faint, and not by character; in fact, that is the defining factor in a great deal of existing law.

Frequent apologies by government and the Waitangi Tribunal have added to the belief that great wrongs have been done and there must be atonement. Maori have been given the opportunity to draft legislation and have been given a special position as the first people to have a say, setting the narrative and determining the resulting policy.

The dominant position is held to be due to their supposed indigenous status (forgetting their antecedents), descendants of people who came many centuries ago to violently drive the existing inhabitants from their lands – as if that far-off history of people long dead should direct the organisation of a twenty-first century developed nation, as if the many lessons of history and the considerable advances brought from across the world have no value. As if people are no longer equal members of the one human race but inherently divided.

I have a friend whose wife has some Maori ancestry; she, and their children, are defined as Maori, he is not. He thus belongs to a different category of citizenship. So, we are all divided, classified, labelled, and treated according to the class of race we belong to. The foundations of a free society are shattered.

A call to return to the past old ways, the traditional culture, *tikanga*, is highlighted. *Tikanga* is to be recovered, to play a determinant role in deciding our collective way of life (for all of us, both Maori and non-Maori) – and this is being achieved.

The picture is blurred, words that guide law, like 'Maori' and '*tikanga*', are never defined and have multiple meanings, so that the application of this thinking is determined by the complainant group alone, to suit a particular purpose. At times, claims are made (incorrectly) for a first people status and that this *tikanga* is the culture of old: surely absurd as there is no apparent desire to reintroduce tribal warfare, cannibalism and slavery. The new form is effectively a mish-mash, an amalgam of the introduced Christianity and European ideals together with selected elements of the pre-contact way of life, one key element being loyalty to the tribe and not to the nation and all the people. The proclaimed division, and the resulting 'partnership' (again, now firmly in place), is a recipe for domination and possible conflict.[224]

This revolution is being carried out by an array of co-operating organisations. There are many *hapu* and *iwi* groups across the country. There is the Maori king movement which started in the Waikato in 1858 and then led a rebellion[225], the Maori Council set up in 1962, the 1987 *Iwi* Leaders' Forum[226], now the *Iwi* Chairs Forum first convened in 2005[227], the political Maori Party and the powerful Maori caucus in Labour Party.

Those groups have considerable power and have been effective within government. Jacinda Ardern is a puppet, a front for Nanaia Mahuta (who has strong links to the king movement). They have been active in formulating major policy initiatives.

The current push for co-governance is based on the proposals of the *He Papua* report to government, which in turn was based on the report of *Matike Mai Aotearoa*, an Independent Working Group on Constitutional Transformation, which was first promoted at a meeting of the *Iwi* Chairs' Forum in 2010. The preparation of *Matike Mai Aotearoa* involved the participation of many Maori organisations. The Chairperson and Convenor facilitated 252 *hui*

---

[224] Robinson 2019
[225] Robinson 2016
[226] Rata 2021
[227] Robinson 2022, pages 58-59

between 2012 and 2015. The *ropu rangatahi* (young people's organisation) that was convened by Veronica Tawhai presented 70 *wananga* (forums). After Cabinet established the *He Puapua* Declaration Working Group in 2019, that Group also invited written submissions, organised focus groups, and conducted one-on-one interviews in "an engagement approach with *iwi, hapu* and *whanau*", **not with all New Zealanders**.[228]

There have been a number of such occasions (under both National and Labour governments), when the development of national policy, which affects all New Zealanders, has been handed over to Maori.

In 1994, when the Office of Treaty Settlements was developing a government process to deal with treaty claims, which surely involve all New Zealanders – we pay for settlements out of our common purse and the rights given to Maori, both local and national, are taken from us - discussions involved Maori only.[229] The consultation process on the settlement process involved twelve regional *hui* – every one on a *marae* – and a national *hui* in the Beehive. These were for Maori, and **not other New Zealanders**, with the clear instruction that "Maori will be invited to send representatives to the national *hui*."[230]

That domination of Maori in policy generation is continuing. In 2022, Maori Development Minister Willie Jackson released feedback **from consultation with Maori** on how New Zealand could implement the United Nations Declaration on the Rights of Indigenous Peoples (UNDRIP) – the blueprint for the breakup of New Zealand. That "initial consultation" involved 69 workshops with 370 Maori participants over six months as the first phase in developing a plan to **support** the declaration; the next step being the drafting of an official plan, and only then – when the policy will have

---

[228] Robinson 2021, page 158
[229] Robinson 2012, page 246
[230] Office of Treaty Settlements 1994

been developed and polished – would there be consultation with the rest of us.[231]

This has been formalised: a new layer of bureaucracy has been created called "regional advisory panels" for councils, with *iwi* appointments alongside elected representatives as well as "regional representative groups", which also require *iwi* appointments (such as the oversight Representative Group made up of local councils and *mana whenua* proposed in the Three Waters legislation).

The extensive scope of activities of Maori organisations has come to include influence on international affairs and active participation in international meetings. The 2005 visit of a Special Rapporteur on the situation of human rights and fundamental freedoms of indigenous peoples, Rodolfo Stavenhagen, was prompted by complaints made by Maori to the United Nations Committee on the Elimination of Racial Discrimination, that the Foreshore and Seabed Act 2004 (passed by the Labour government, and criticised by the National opposition as giving too many special rights to Maori) discriminated against Maori. He was **not** invited by the New Zealand Government, which was not pleased by the suggestion from this international organisation that (among others) the Foreshore and Seabed Act should be repealed or amended.[232]

A 2019 visit from an Expert Mechanism on the Rights of Indigenous Peoples (EMRIP) Country Engagement Mission came at the invitation of a Maori organisation: in response to a request from the *Aotearoa* **Independent Monitoring Mechanism** (AIMM) on behalf of the **National** *Iwi* **Chairs Forum** and the New Zealand Human Rights Commission.[233]

---

[231] https://www.rnz.co.nz/news/te-manu-korihi/465708/government-begins-drafting-indigenous-rights-plan
[232] Stavenhagen 2005; Adcock 2012, page 99; Robinson 2021, pages 48-52
[233] Robinson 2021, pages 57-58

Maori are also playing a separate role in the formulation of international policies, such as the organisation of international trade. A Maori body, *Nga Toki Whakarururanga* was set up in late 2020, to enable effective Maori influence on trade negotiations. The proposed roles for *Nga Toki Whakarururanga* included being able to: "Develop processes of engagement that enable Maori as the *Tiriti*/Treaty partner to exercise genuine influence over trade policy, broadly defined, including at various stages of decision making in negotiations for international trade and investment agreements."[234]

Involvement in official foreign relations continued when, in 2021, the *Iwi* Chairs Forum partnered with the New Zealand Government to develop *Te Aratini* for Expo 2020 Dubai, the first ever Festival of Indigenous and Tribal Ideas at a World Expo.[235]

Two important national conferences followed in 2022, both designed to push forward the idea of Maori exceptionalism and co-governance – not to raise questions or to open up the debate. On 4 July, Diplosphere ("a non-partisan think tank which aims to promote independent thinking and diplomacy"), with the support of the New Zealand National Commission for UNESCO, organised the "First national conference on Maori perspectives on the great international issues of our time": "Navigating a stormy world; *Te ao Maori* perspectives; Anchoring Maori values in foreign policy".[236] This was to be guided by *Tirohanga Maori* (the Maori world view) with discussion led by "*iwi*, business, academic, and youth leaders". "The conference raises the question: What does 'Western values' mean in *Aotearo*a New Zealand of 2022? It will explore the cultural, trade,

---

[234] Joint press release by Waitangi Tribunal Claimants and the Ministry of Foreign Affairs and Trade. https://www.mfat.govt.nz/en/media-and-resources/joint-press-release-by-waitangi-tribunal-claimants-and-the-ministry-of-foreign-affairs-and-trade/
[235] https://www.stuff.co.nz/pou-tiaki/300438502/iwi-leaders-to-drive-world-expos-first-ever-festival-of-indigenous-and-tribal-ideas
[236] https://www.diplosphere.org/conference

and political links that have long existed between Maori and the Asia Pacific region, and what the future holds."

In November, 2022, there is the Constitutional Conference Korero at Auckland University, a national *hui* "to provide the technical and legal support for constitutional transformation in *Aotearoa* New Zealand. The conference will bring together 'experts' from around *Aotearoa* and the world, to offer practical and pragmatic legal advice on options for constitutional transformation, grounded in models for constitutional transformation that were proposed in the 2016 report of *Matike Mai Aotearoa*. ... The conference will give Maori, *Matike Mai Aotearoa*, the wider public and the New Zealand Government opportunities to engage with legal and academic experts on constitutional law and Indigenous rights. ... The 'Constitutional Korero' will be a once-in-a decade national *wananga* bringing together experts from around the world and within *Aotearoa* to present arguments and options for constitutional transformation to realise Maori rights in *te Tiriti o Waitangi*, *He Whakaputanga* and the UN Declaration on the Rights of Indigenous Peoples."[237]

The Auckland University Medical School says it needs to address "the terrible inequities suffered by Maori and Pacifica" with an admission scheme which sets apart 30% of entries for Maori and Pacifica students. The new Maori Health Authority, unsurprisingly, supports the University's approach. Other students are unhappy that positive discrimination allows Maori to enter the course with lesser qualifications. They have struggled and work hard, and seen many of their hard-working fellow students fail entry requirements, while some others get in on lesser (race-based) standards of accreditation.

TVNZ has approached this issue with a one-sided and emotional report of racist abuse to the Maori students, interviewing two complaining students and reporting a number of distasteful emails – as if such extreme attacks are typical of the attitudes of the wider

---

[237] constitutionalkorero2022@auckland.ac.nz

student body. There is no indication of the wider issues raised by this discrimination.[238]

The division by race and the widespread special treatment of Maori has engendered a feeling of being owed something, of entitlement, of being a chosen people, and of arrogance – which is displayed in a refusal to listen to any contrary points of view, and resulted in aggressive behaviour. Unfriendly feelings are often evident, and were made particularly clear at the meeting with the Human Rights Commission, and the Waitangi Tribunal hearing, both referred to above.

The silencing of dissent to their ideology is supported by the current government which effectively controls the media, with a requirement for funding of "commitment to *Te Tiriti o Waitangi* and to Maori as a *Te Tiriti* partner"[239], and an attempt to ban 'hate speech' which sets down the context for creating a socially cohesive society in Aotearoa New Zealand as being "underpinned by *Te Tiriti o Waitangi, Te Ao Maori* perspectives and the Maori-Crown relationship".[240] Refutation of that re-invented Treaty, and insistence on equality, is outlawed in the media.

The initial proposal concerning hate speech included a requirement that closely paralleled early South African apartheid legislation: "This change would make it against the law for someone to incite others to discriminate against a protected group."[241] The example above of admissions to the Auckland University Medical School shows that meanwhile discrimination against the non-protected non-Maori is admissible.

---

[238] TVNZ 6 pm news 31 May.
https://www.youtube.com/watch?v=vpn6TOe5E60
[239] Robinson 2021, page 8
[240] Government press release, *Social Cohesion Programme to Address Incitement of Hatred and Discrimination*
[241] Scoop Independent News 2021; Robinson 2021, page 15

Extremist Maori have been emboldened to take part in intimidation and bullying actions.[242] There has been the way that Prime Minister Helen Clark was reduced to tears at Waitangi in 1998, the control of meetings and violent action against unwanted speakers, the 79-day occupation of Moutoa Gardens in Whanganui to force a favourable settlement of a Treaty of Waitangi claim, the two-year occupation of land owned by Fletcher Building, which prevented a much-needed development from going ahead (negotiations with the Maori king resulted in the 2020 government purchase of the land for *papakainga* [Maori], housing for *mana whenua* (traditional owners) and some public housing) – and much more.

An extreme case of such aggressive behaviour was in 2007 when a Maori group were gathering weapons, dressing in camouflage gear, often hiding their identities and training in bush camps in the Ureweras for armed combat.[243] As the judge commented when making sentence on four leaders found guilty of firearms charges: "As I view the evidence, in effect, a private militia was being established. Whatever the justification, that is a frightening prospect in our society, undermining of our democratic institutions and anathema to our way of life."[244] A remarkable feature of the situation was the outcry and criticism of Police action (which had been to protect New Zealand from potential terrorism) from the media and politicians, resulting in a 2004 Police apology to the Ruatoki community and the Tuhoe people "for the wrongdoing that occurred during *Te Urewera* raids" – but there was no apology for practising armed combat.

In June, 2022, the government announced that they had set up 'The Centre of Research Excellence for Preventing and Countering Violent Extremism, *He Whenua Taurikura*'. This is to implement a recommendation of the Royal Commission of Inquiry report into the

---

[242] Robinson 2019, pages 158-173; Robinson 2021, pages 12-15
[243] Robinson 2012, pages 256-257
[244] Sentencing notes of Rodney Hansen J. [47] 24 May 2012

terrorist attack on Christchurch masjidain.[245] There is no recognition of the home-grown terrorism threatened by the exercises in the Ureweras: nor is there any awareness of the extremism of Maori demands and intentions.

Part of this strategy is the game of 'non-violent' protest, whereby demonstrators are allowed to break the law, to occupy land not theirs, and to interfere with the freedom of others, with impunity. There is no violence so long as they are left alone to flout the law. But efforts to apply the law and to protect the rights of others are met with cries of violence – and then with violence from the demonstrators. Illegal occupation has long been part of Maori tactics, used from Parihaka in 1881[246] to the present day.

Bureaucrats, politicians and ordinary citizens have learned from the bullying to keep their heads down, not to raise questions and to let it all happen. The nation has been ripped apart. The fruits of the separatist ideology and the determination to seize power are evident now, and soon to be much worse unless the movement is stopped and New Zealand turns back towards a unified nation of equal citizens.

This country is broken, increasingly divided into two, distinct groups with completely separate, different rights, different treatment. Some examples have been mentioned.

- Maori threaten to disrupt a speaker, and do so, and the speaker is attacked as being racist for raising concerns and upsetting them.
- Police carry out justified raids to seize weapons from training terrorists and are forced to apologise.
- Maori students get special treatment and when competing students raise concerns, they are labelled 'racist'.

---

[245] https://www.beehive.govt.nz/release/centre-preventing-and-countering-violent-extremism-officially-open
[246] McLean 2020

- A call made on national television to ban books is supported by those in authority; no one cares.

In addition, an alternative Maori government is set up and claims authority, and the government agency takes no action (see below).

A particularly disturbing example of the ruthless abuse of power, and of judicial persecution, is the case of Northland farmer, Allan Titford who (in 1986) found his life destroyed by Maori activism.[247] There was a series of attacks on his property, his house and bulldozers were damaged, a cottage destroyed, squatters on his land, a fence pulled down.

Claims on Titford's property were considered to be unfounded by a number of authorities, and in 1988 Prime Minister David Lange wrote to Titford that the Minister of Justice, Geoffrey Palmer, had done a search through the Lands and Deeds Office and confirmed that the land in dispute was indisputably owned by Allan in fee simple. Yet in 1989 the Waitangi Tribunal began hearings on the claim, following which "the Crown agreed to a 'statement of fact' with Te Roroa that 'the lands known as *Manuwhetai* and *Whangaiariki* had been taken in error by the Crown'."

Under the multiple pressures of those turbulent years, Titford's marriage broke apart. His wife brought new, uncorroborated, claims of rape and he received the outrageous sentence of a non-parole period of 24 years imprisonment. Titford was in the same bind that faced Peter Ellis, who refused to attend parole board hearings while in prison (1993-2000) because he would have to confess to the crimes in order to argue for early release; there is no chance of parole while the accused continues to insist on his innocence. Titford was an ordinary person and, like you and I in such circumstances, was bewildered by what was done to him. He is still in jail.

---

[247] Butler 2018; Robinson 2019, pages 163-164

Tribalism triumphant: the *He Puapua* tsunami

If there is one master in the house, all is peace; if there are two masters, all is confusion. The same with the land of New Zealand. The land is not big enough for two kings.
Sir John Hall (Premier of New Zealand, 1879 to 1882), 1860

When the full intention became clear in 2021, when the public was made aware of the *He Puapua* report to government, the minority Maori proposal for a fundamental constitutional transformation and the complete overthrow of our Westminster form of government came as a shock to most New Zealanders.

Here was a bombshell, an announcement of the takeover by an extremist, separatist, and racist, ideology.

The report, which was based on the *Matike mai* report for the *Iwi Chairs' Forum* and the contradictory, muddled United Nations Declaration on the Rights of Indigenous Peoples (UNDRIP), was written in 2019 and then kept secret during the 2020 elections; the Labour Party certainly understood that such proposals would not have majority support, so they proceeded by stealth. Knowledge of what was going on came only with a question in Parliament from the ACT opposition party. In 2021 and 2022 efforts were continuing to ram the key proposals through a subservient, one-chamber, parliament before the public could have a determining say in the next 2023 elections.

That declaration, UNDRIP, has clearly been written by a committee who do not agree amongst themselves; indeed, it presents two completely opposed points of view. It commences with a clear statement of equality (quoted at the beginning of this book) but then goes on to argue for the division and special rights that are condemned here. This Government has seized the wrong end of the stick, following the call for racial division and ignoring that initial call for the equality that is a founding principle of the United Nations.

As outlined in the previous chapter 'A nation divided', a great deal has been done already to give Maori disproportionate rights; *He Puapua* set down a considerable list of further steps in that direction.

"The proposed division of power is extensive. An idea of the scope of the comprehensive division, and the special privileges to Maori, can be gained from a few examples.

- Maori should have 'the ability to exercise full authority over our lands, waters and natural resources'.

- 'Self determination' will include 'self-government arrangements and autonomous authority in agreed areas (e.g. independent indigenous education systems and healthcare services)'.

- '*Tikanga Maori* will be functioning and applicable across Aotearoa under Maori (national, *iwi, hapu, whanau*) authority'.

- 'co-governance might entail a joint governance structure, or it might involve mechanisms for the respective governance entities to co-ordinate to make law and policy'. Note here the assumption of two separate bodies forming national law.

- 'We have suggested a phased approach to engagement with Maori' (page 12), with 'an engagement process with *iwi, hapu* and *whanau*', so that the development of the Plan will ensure that 'a broad section of Maori participate in and are consulted throughout this process'. There is much talk of direct Maori involvement, none of other New Zealanders, who are largely absent from this Plan.

- 'transfer services and jurisdiction over key areas to *iwi, hapu* and *whanau* (including health, state care and criminal justice)'.

Many common activities, such as education, health, law and criminal justice, are to be split up, with defining power to Maori. There is, however, no talk of any separate funding. It appears that the majority of the population will fund the whole system; Maori will have their 'autonomous' systems but not the responsibility to provide for themselves."[248]

The extent of the intended constitutional transformation is made plain in *He Puapua* by a descriptive chart, with its origins clearly stated: "Drawing on the report *Matike Mai Aotearoa*, the *He Puapua* Declaration Working Group has adopted a *Tiriti* model [a '*Te Tiriti/Rangatiratanga* Framework'] based round 'spheres of authority'."[249]

The goal for 2040 is for two racially defined parliaments, the *Tikanga Maori* House for Maori and the *Tikanga Pakeha* House for all others, overseen by a Treaty of Waitangi House for Maori and *Pakeha*, where there would be a Maori veto.[250]

This plan of a complete transformation, indeed a complete destruction, of the New Zealand constitution, system of government and way of life, has been building for some time. That idea of a triple parliament had been suggested, and refused, in a 2000 'Building the Constitution Conference', organised by the Institute of Policy Studies (Victoria University), and held in the Legislative Chamber of Parliament.[251] "The Maori viewpoint included a presentation by Whata Winiata proposing two parliaments (the *Tikanga Maori* House for Maori and the *Tikanga Pakeha* House for others) oversean by a Treaty of Waitangi House for Maori and *Pakeha*. A Maori veto is asserted: 'Assenting and voting in the Treaty house will be by *tikanga*. Any decision will require a majority of the Crown/*tikanga*

---

[248] Robinson 2021, pages 70-71
[249] Working Group 2019, page vi
[250] Robinson 2021, pages 72-76
[251] James 2000

Pakeha representatives and a majority of the *tikanga Maori* representatives.'"[252]

The government has taken quick action to follow the prescriptions of *He Puapua*.

- The right of ratepayers to call for a poll when Maori wards are proposed for local councils (which have always succeeded to block the separate representation) has been removed by dictate of the Minister, Nanaia Mahuta.

- A Maori Health Authority (to work with *Iwi*-Maori Partnership Boards, Maori health providers, *iwi*, *hapu* and Maori communities) has been set up.

- The Ministry of Education is undertaking a revision of all curricula with the clear intention to honour our past and supposed obligations to the re-invented version of the Treaty.

- The 'Three Waters' Plan is to take valuable assets built up over many years by councils – the infrastructure and control of water systems – into central government control. After more than 60 *iwi*-only meetings, the Government and tribal leaders have divided New Zealand into four massive, unwieldy zones, with the top tier of the structure in each zone taking ownership and control of the water and water-related infrastructure. The only say for councils will be to choose half (six members) of a Regional Representative Group; the other half will be tribal representatives chosen (in some unspecified fashion) by the dominant *iwi* of the region. The whole system will be guided by "a dedicated water services regulator for *Aotearoa*", *Taumata Arowai*, which "will operate from a *te ao Maori* perspective.[253] There has been widespread dismay over that policy, but when it was introduced in Parliament, the Water Services Entities Bill 2022 kept the co-

---

[252] Robinson 2021, pages 87-88
[253] Robinson 2021, pages 134-139

governance, the racial division of power, and retained the "equal number of territorial representatives and *mana whenua* representatives", with many requirements supposedly driven by the Treaty of Waitangi, such as "the board of each water services entity must respond to *Te Mana o te Wai* statements for water services issued to the entity by *mana whenua*".[254] That split was always fundamental to the new legislation.

The intention is that the public is to get used to this fundamental division of power; the next step towards the complete assertion of apartheid with a racially divided parliament is to demand acceptance of co-governance – already existing in many ways – as a fundamental feature of New Zealand society.

---

[254] online on Water Services Entities Bill websites

Co-governance – constitutional transformation based on race

It was, and is, constitutionally impossible for the Crown to enter into a partnership with her subjects. By definition, the Crown is supreme, and the people are subject to her laws.
Former Judge and Law Lecturer, Anthony Willy

The chiefs placed in the hands of the Queen of England the sovereign authority forever, and the embodiment of that authority is now in the New Zealand Parliament. For that reason, any demands for Maori authorities, are nothing more than wishful thinking.
Apirana Ngata

Co-governance is to split the country in two, and to throw away the supreme power of Parliament, of one people and for one people. On one side are those with a bit of Maori ancestry. The multitude, all the rest, form the second-class citizenry. It's as simple as that.

This plan is well advanced. Following the *He Puapua* report, in July 2021 the Minister for Maori Development, Willie Jackson, announced "the next steps in developing a national plan to implement the United Nations Declaration on the Rights of Indigenous Peoples". The procedure has become all too familiar – "Government will consult with Maori over the next few months before engaging with the wider public on indigenous rights, in the wake of *He Puapua* controversy."[255] Maori first, all others second.

While this government is acting to **implement** this international accord, there has been no parliamentary consideration of, or approval

---

[255] https://www.newshub.co.nz/home/politics/2021/07/united-nations-declaration-indigenous-rights-consultation-begins-in-wake-of-he-puapua-controversy.html

for, the United Nations Declaration on the Rights of Indigenous Peoples. This was a matter decided by the Executive and it was not a decision made by Parliament; authorisation seems to have been given by Cabinet to supporting the declaration. Successive governments, National and Labour, have acted to sign up to, and conform to, a controversial international declaration without any consideration by the public or Parliament.

On 22 and 23 March, 2022, Prime Minister Jacinda Ardern confirmed that public consultation on Maori co-governance would happen that year[256], and Jackson provided further information.

"In 2018 the government commissioned a report on potential co-governance arrangements with Maori. But since receiving the *He Puapua* report in 2019, it has constantly denied that its proposals represented government policy or intent. Indeed, it was only after much goading that it even admitted the report's existence, and it was not until the middle of last year that a redacted version was publicly released.

But last week, with little fanfare, the Prime Minister acknowledged at a media conference, almost as an aside, that the government was working on advancing co-governance proposals and would be carrying out public consultation on its plans later this year. She offered no further details on the scope of any co-governance arrangements, the form of the public consultation, or what the government's endgame was.

The following day, Maori Development Minister Willie Jackson spelled out the government's intentions in more detail. He said organisations including the New Zealand Maori Council, the Maori Women's Welfare League, and other unnamed but 'significant' Maori and *iwi* groups and leaders (but apparently no

---

[256] https://www.newshub.co.nz/home/politics/2022/03/prime-minister-jacinda-ardern-confirms-public-consultation-on-m-ori-co-governance-will-happen-in-2022.html

Pakeha organisations or individuals) were being tasked with developing a plan for co-governance. He would then take the plan to Cabinet for approval, before its release to the public for general consultation."[257]

Other reports gave a different list of the organisations which would be involved: "He said the next step would be the drafting of an official plan – work which would be done by *Te Puni Kokiri*, the National *Iwi* Chairs Forum's *Pou Tikanga* and the Human Rights Commission - over the next couple of months."[258]

Jackson outlined the feedback from consultation with Maori: "'The feedback has been that there are many ways we can strengthen indigenous rights and achieve better outcomes for all ... For example there are some innovative *iwi*-led housing initiatives which are making a huge difference in communities and the revitalisation of *te reo Maori* is another area this government has supported which aligns with UNDRIP.' Feedback largely focused on several topics but strengthening *tino rangatiratanga* for *tangata whenua* was most consistently raised, as a central theme for discussions ranging from health, justice and education, to protecting *te taiao* (environment) and *te reo Maori*. It included calls for independent *kaupapa Maori* educational institutions, and a Maori health authority to address inequities, the importance of *te reo Maori*, supporting an economic basis for Maori entrepreneurship, safeguarding land and resources, improving education about indigenous rights and *Te Tiriti o Waitangi*, improvements in the justice system, solving housing problems, and supporting the wellbeing of families." Note the complete absence of non-Maori here; this is the viewpoint of a racially defined minority.

---

[257] https://www.newsroom.co.nz/maori-co-governance-deserves-better-than-a-bitter-and-divisive-public-debate
[258] https://www.rnz.co.nz/news/te-manu-korihi/465708/government-begins-drafting-indigenous-rights-plan

The report, "Targeted engagement with Maori on declaration plan"[259], provided no further information.

Jackson said that, while the Government has adopted some ideas from *He Puapua*, it has ruled out other ideas, such as a separate Maori Parliament. "*He Puapua* is not the Declaration Plan, nor is it Government policy ... Reports like *He Puapua* and *Matike Mai* are part of a long history of reports on addressing Indigenous rights in Aotearoa and should be seen in that context."

Many remain unconvinced; many share the feeling that this Labour government is not to be trusted; they may have said that they don't want those separate governments **just now**, but all their policies are moving exactly in that direction. We are asked to follow through the murky mist, meekly giving up our own country.

In May, 2021, National leader Judith Collins had questioned Prime Minister Jacinda Ardern's ruling out of a separate Maori Parliament, brushing off that denial as 'spin'. Collins called for a "national conversation" about recommendations made in *He Puapua*, "that sets out a roadmap to co-governance between the Crown and Maori by 2040".[260] In March, 2022, ACT leader David Seymour announced that a referendum on Maori co-governance – which he likened to an 'unequal society' – was a bottom line for any coalition negotiations in 2023.[261]

Meanwhile, non-government organisations have been organising conferences to develop the proposal for constitutional change. As already noted, on July 4, 2022, Diplosphere, with the support of the New Zealand National Commission for UNESCO, organised the "First national conference on Maori perspectives on the great

---

[259] file:///C:/Users/User/Downloads/tpk-undrip-targeted-2022.pdf
[260] https://www.newshub.co.nz/home/politics/2021/05/national-leader-judith-collins-questions-prime-minister-jacinda-ardern-s-ruling-out-of-separate-m-ori-parliament.html
[261] https://www.1news.co.nz/2022/03/24/act-party-wants-referendum-on-co-governance-with-maori/

international issues of our time". In November, 2022, there will be a Constitutional Conference *Korero* at Auckland University, a national *hui* "to provide the technical and legal support for constitutional transformation in *Aotearoa* New Zealand." where experts "will present arguments and options for constitutional transformation to realise Maori rights in *te Tiriti o Waitangi*, *He Whakaputanga* and the UN Declaration on the Rights of Indigenous Peoples."[262] (see previous chapter 'A ruthless ideology')

The full meaning of 'co-governance', and just how far the government really means to go, remains unclear. Indeed, the lack of clarity appears to be a deliberate policy. Meanwhile, the idea of co-governance, splitting of the country into two apartheid-like racial groups, has enthusiastic support from key government Ministers (Mahuta and Little) and even some in the National Party.

In intemperate comments to the online magazine *E-Tangata*, former National Treaty Minister Christopher Finlayson has described those opposed to co-governance as "the KKK brigade", reinforcing the widespread public perception that the slightest public opposition to the proposed changes will bring down accusations of racism upon the opponent's head. "The people I call 'the KKK brigade' are out there. They dream of a world that never was, and never could be. ... They don't really understand *tangata whenua*. They don't like change. There are always going to be people like that, and you have to be reasonably charitable towards them for a while – and then just ignore them and get on with things."[263]

This is nonsense. The KKK fight **for** racism, for different treatment based on race. As, indeed, does the co-governance policy. The opponents of separation are the **enemies** of the believers in that KKK doctrine of racial division – people like Finlayson.

---

[262] constitutionalkorero2022@auckland.ac.nz
[263] https://e-tangata.co.nz/comment-and-analysis/chris-finlayson-co-governance-should-be-embraced-not-feared/

What does co-governance imply?

- the end of equality, of being one people,
- the complete destruction of democracy, in which each adult has an equal vote in the one electorate,
- overthrow of our whole way of government.

Why should this be an option?

- 'Maori are *tangata whenua*, indigenous people' – untrue and irrelevant,
- 'Maori have suffered from colonisation and reparations are called for' – false,
- 'existing inequalities cry out for separation' – a failure to recognise past success and the recent causes of differences, of class.

The idea of co-governance remains unclear, with further policies being developed by the very Maori groups that commissioned *Matike Mai*, which formed the blueprint for *He Papua*. The series of 'consultations' – not involving the majority of New Zealanders – appears as a smokescreen, hiding a very real agenda that the proponents know would be unpopular if the public understood what is happening. There is to be no referendum while the social fabric of New Zealand is ripped apart, forced through by the effective dictatorship of only one house of parliament, with no checks and balances. Co-governance promises more of the same, with a constitutional transformation that denies equity and is based on racial division.

The final step, the ultimate goal is that set out in *He Puapua*; here is their picture of the future of New Zealand in 2040, the division of parliament, the end of the Westminster system.[264] If co-governance means something, this is it.

Diagram 1 of *He Puapua* (right side): *Rangatiratanga* / Joint / *Kawanatanga* Spheres. 2040

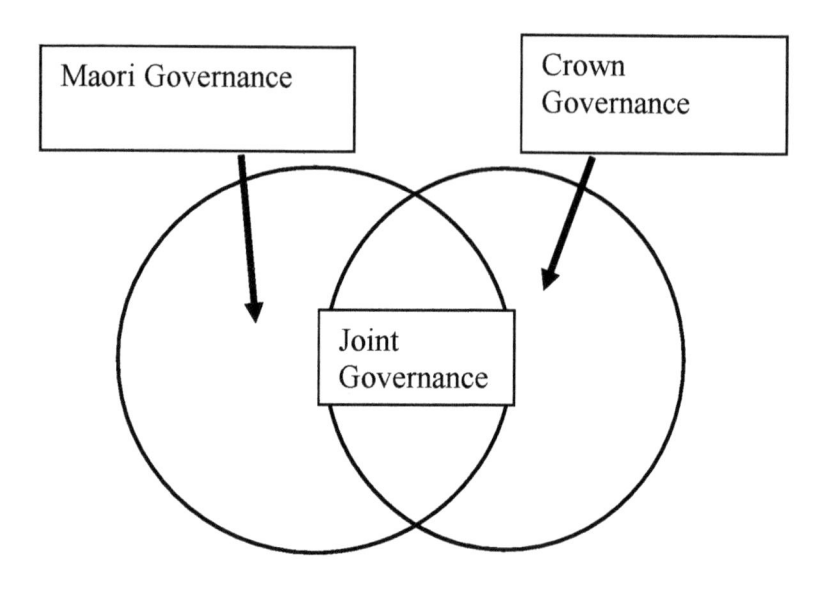

```
    Maori Governance              Crown
                                  Governance
              ↓               ↓

                  Joint
                  Governance
```

- One government, the 'Crown', is for all of us, with no intention that Maori will withdraw, and no suggestion of the end of Maori seats.

- Equal authority will be exercised by the Maori government, led by a chiefly elite, *rangatira*, under the *tikanga* principle of *rangatiratanga*. The mass of Maori will gain little, if anything, from that seizure of power.

---

[264] Robinson 2021, page 75

- The joint meeting-place, to settle differences between the two centres of power, will an effective Maori veto.

This juggernaut, the tsunami promised by *He Puapua*, **will continue unless it stopped by determined and forceful action.**

An existing separate Maori government

New Zealand has been steadily moving towards the breakup of unified government. A number of Maori organisations control key resources and have taken action on the international stage, and more is intended.

A number of such recent steps have been described above. One significant example is the 2022 legislation on Three Waters, where the choice of regional entities (controlling and owning the resources) is made through a series of stages, starting with 'Regional Representation Groups' that are half chosen by local authorities and half by *'mana whenua'*. As previously noted, there is no clarity concerning who decides policy and organises the group representing *mana whenua*. **Yet these undefined tribal groupings are given the authority and responsibilities of government; they are required by the legislation to set policy and to make appointments. They are not only allowed to set up a de facto alternate government; they are, in fact, instructed to do so.** That division is a feature of current government policy of co-governance, which is moving firmly towards the complete separation of government set down in *He Puapua* for 2040

Others have not waited but have formed their version of the proposed alternative government already. When I discovered an osteopath who was operating illegally, practising without being properly registered, I found that her website made the claim that she "is a WHC registered osteopath". She required patients to sign an indemnity clause in a five-page contract before treating them, including: "Our practitioners shall be immune from prosecution or censure by any authority, person, or entity, insofar as they are acting within the above stated principles, laws, and precepts in the context of their acknowledged skill set that has been vetted by the

Wakaminenga Health Council (WHC) as part of their registration. The *Wakaminenga* Health Council shall be the sole authority to which our health practitioners are accountable."

This *Wakaminenga* Health Council is claimed to be authorised by the "Maori government of *Aotearoa nu tireni*". Here is the claim of authority held by an alternative, Maori government. I took a complaint to Osteopaths New Zealand Inc, who referred me on to the Osteopathic Council of New Zealand, who referred me on to the Ministry of Health, who are the appropriate authority for taking action.

The response showed that the authorities were well aware of the infringements. "The Ministry is aware of '*Wakaminenga Kaunihera Hauora* Health Council', and the 'Maori Government of *Aotearoa Nu Tireni*' and **is actively considering options** to respond to their claims to be able to issue Annual Practising Certificates to health practitioners. In regards to the osteopath, the Ministry **is making enquiries** into their compliance with section 7 of the Health Practitioners Competence Assurance Act (2003)."[265]

That was May 7, 2022. I persisted and sent a further email asking whether they were doing anything, asking three explicit questions. On 16 June there were no answers, only a question whether I want these questions to be treated as a request under the Official Information Act – with a comment about good reasons for withholding official information, telling me that this would be a waste of time, but I made that request. The reply, dated 14 July, 2022, told nothing: "The matters that you raise are currently subject to an ongoing legal proceeding that is before the court. As such, your request is refused in full."

I had passed this information to the ACT Party, who raised this issue with the Ministry, who replied in similar words: "The Ministry is

---

[265] email to the author from Principal Advisor, Enforcement, Ministry of Health, May 7

aware of '*Wakaminenga Kaunihera Hauora* Health Council', and the 'Maori Government of *Aotearoa Nu Tireni*'. I can advise that actions are underway by the Ministry but the Ministry cannot disclose any further detail at this time."

The several authorities were afraid to face up to Maori treason (this is exactly what this, the setting up of a separate government) and were kicking for touch. Otherwise, action would have been prompt and decisive.

Throughout, I have been told that I have the facts right, that there is an infraction, but that no-one is going to do anything about it; they are able to break the law with impunity. This is a common experience; New Zealanders are afraid of Maori, and Maori can flout the law. I have often been shown to be naïve in my expectations that we should all obey the law, and that any infractions will be dealt with promptly. While those in authority support Maori exceptionalism, many New Zealanders are unhappy, but all too often reasonable argument is met with a media focus on the Maori position, and claims of racism.

The website of "*Te Wakaminenga* Maori government of *Aotearoa nu tireni*: the de jure Government of the Chiefs of the Confederation of the Maori Tribes" (with a Te Awamutu box number address) provides further information on this alternative government.[266]

Here is the claim to be "the lawful government of *Aotearoa nu tireni*, recognised under international law since October 28, 1835", in a proclamation dated 14 February 14, 2022, which was sent to the World Health Organisation, signed by 'Prime Minister' Arikinui Ripekatangi (Georgina Job).[267] There is no stated connection with other Maori organisations.

They announce that this proclamation "shall also serve as a pre-emptive notice that we reject all attempts of the corporation known

---

[266] https://govt.maori.nz/
[267] op cit, news sheet

as Her Majesty Queen [sic] in right of New Zealand and Crown Corporation, or any other entity or corporation to usurp control of our *whenua rangatira* any present or future treaties with the World Health Organisation, United Nations and any other foreign entities or otherwise." That refutation of the New Zealand government, with a decision to "freely choose to abandon the aforementioned NZ Corporation and give our full support to the sovereign nation of *Aotearoa Nu Tireni* and its representatives and elected government", is repeated in a further website.[268]

If this is not treason, then what is?

The 'Confederation of the Maori Tribes' (noted previously) and the date of 'October 28, 1835' are references to a letter drafted by the Consular Agent and British Resident, James Busby, and signed by thirty-four northern Maori chiefs at his residence in Waitangi; this is often referred to as *'He Wakaputanga'*. Despite the heading ("Declaration of the Independence of New Zealand*")* this letter was not a true declaration but rather a statement of intent. The third article of the letter makes this clear: "The hereditary chiefs and heads of tribes agree to meet in Congress at Waitangi in the autumn of each year, for the purpose of framing laws for the dispensation of justice, the preservation of peace and good order, and the regulation of trade; and they cordially invite the Southern tribes to lay aside their private animosities and to consult the safety and welfare of our common country, by joining the Confederation of the United Tribes."[269]

No such meetings took place. Busby failed to convene any further such gatherings and "warfare had again broken out in the north between rival alliances of *hapu*, dashing hopes for an annual congress of chiefs."[270] The proposal was not presented to other tribes, and that

---

[268] https://govt.maori.nz/overview/
[269] Robinson 2015, pages 67-71
[270] Department of Internal Affairs 2017, page 23

effort failed. The intended national authority never came into being, and the claim for authority based on it is fraudulent.

This fake *Wakaminenga* government offers a "Protected individual Vaccine exception" card, exempting a person "from receiving any vaccine or medical tests which breach *hapu tikanga* customary laws".[271]

They also provide a trespass order, proclaiming: "WARNING TRESPASS NOTICE! TO ALL NEW ZEALAND GOVERNMENT OR LOCAL COUNCIL REPRESENTATIVES, POLICE, MILITARY OR OFFICERS OF Her Majesty the Queen in Right of New Zealand or Corporate representatives. YOU MAY NOT ENTER WITHOUT CONSENT".[272]

The claim is that: "The flag herein this notice, and that is situated on this Private Land, affirms this property and its occupants are under the jurisdictional authority and protection of *Nga Rangatira o Nga Hapu o Te Wakaminenga o Nu Tireni, Aotearoa* (Congress of Māori Chiefs) who act under the authority of *He Wakaputanga* 1835 also known as the Declaration of Independence 1835. Failure to understand or recognise what this means is not an excuse to breach this authority. ...

The occupants here on this land are protected under *He Wakaputanga* 1835 and Common Law jurisdiction and have not entered into or agreed to a contract of engagement with the New Zealand Government also known as 'Her Majesty the Queen in Right of New Zealand' or any other Council or Corporate entity. TRESPASS DAMAGES shall apply if YOU step onto this Private Property. Minimum Penalty – NZD $10,000.00 (Ten Thousand New Zealand Dollars)."

---

[271] https://govt.maori.nz/wp-content/uploads/2022/05/ADULT-EXEMPTION-CARD-VACCINE-300x186-1.png
[272] https://govt.maori.nz/wp-content/uploads/2022/07/trespass.pdf

In 2018, this 'government' sent a petition to the 'Tax Working Group Secretariat', with copies to a wide range of others, including the Chief Justice, Her Majesty the Queen, His Holiness Pope Francis, the British Lord Chief Justice, Governor-General Patsy Reddy, the United Nations Secretariat of the Permanent Forum on Indigenous Issues, the Prime Minister and a number of Ministers, their 'Maori Government Treasury' and the 'Maniapoto Tribal Government'.[273]

The petition asked for "our percentage of the Gross Domestic Product allocated specifically for the upholding our own *mana* and *tino rangatiratanga* maintaining our rights to self-determination and self-government under our constitutional documents" – "we would like a fairer share of the tax revenue and gross domestic product, transparency, accountability, and treaty auditing of the revenues, royalties, and capital flows off our natural resources, lands, people, local government, customs exports, immigration, etc. due to the extreme poverty, deprivation, homelessness, neglect, inequity, and structural discrimination against *tangata whenua*/maori / native/indigenous people in housing, labour markets, economy, health, education bought [sic] about by neo liberal policies and 180 years of systematic colonial socio-economic and hegemonic oppression."

This extraordinary claim was a request for money gathered by the true government (which they consider illegitimate) to be handed to their alternative government. The Government is still taking no evident action about their various actions, having told me only that it is 'considering options' (noted above).

A series of 'seminars' by speaker Antionette James have been organised across New Zealand (including at Taupo, Waihi, Tauranga,

---

[273] https://taxpolicy.ird.govt.nz/-/media/project/ir/tp/publications/2020/2020-tax-working-group/submissions/twg-subm-3983272-maori-government-of-aotearoa-4-of-4-pdf.pdf?sc_lang=enandmodified=20200910074632andhash=E6CE15C9B0D6C0 6111BE3172F50619FE

Turangi, Christchurch, Gore and Wanaka, plus several public ZOOM meetings).[274] A number of these talks are available on their website; the following notes relate to that at Taupo.

An early quote, with the words of Thomas Jefferson, suggests a priority of individual 'rights' over collective, community government: "Nothing is unchangeable but the inherent and unalienable rights of man." Those rights are then described as "the laws of nature and of nature's god". That concept, which has also wrongly been called 'common law', can be defined as "the rules of moral conduct implanted by nature in the human mind, forming the proper basis for and being superior to all written laws; the will of God revealed to man through his conscience."

Much of the talk followed the spiritual paths of many thinkers in past centuries, before paying particular attention to the activities of the Pope, including during the Second World War. The religious focus continues with a slide of the Jesuit Oath. There is no reference to the New Zealand experience, to either British intentions or to the realities of *tikanga*.

Some three-quarters of the way through, we learn of their health council, which has so concerned me. The actions of authorities, which I could not be told of by the Ministry (see above), are described, as follows: Police phoned their 'Prime Minister' Georgina Job for a dialogue and after some meetings the problem was 'sorted'. The conclusion reached by the group was that: "we were recognised because we are lawful". Further: "we are an authority that is recognised"; the speaker also claimed that they were internationally recognised. Their belief was that their activities were to "make community decisions for our community", with separate jurisdictions, "Maori and non-Maori with different councils being built at the moment". These could then communicate through the media.

---

[274] https://www.facebook.com/antoinettejamesFreedomNZ/

The New Zealand Government has done nothing to counter unlawful activities and that claim for independent sovereignty, only holding talks behind closed doors (with a refusal of information to the ordinary citizen) and leaving lawbreakers untouched, giving them the impression that they have been recognised as legitimate. Meanwhile, this break-away group is acting to destroy the unity of a common community.

Antionette James made their intentions clear in an interview. "We are trying to build up councils so that we can take over ... some councils, we will just man those, others we will just go in and we will deconstruct in significant areas ... Under customary law, we are guardians of the land, and that buys into Judeo-Christian beliefs that we are stewards; we are in control" [275]

This suggests even more than the co-governance proposed by *He Puapua*.

It is all too easy to become confused about just what is going on, as with two further groups I came across, which at first appeared to be all part of that Maori alternative government, until a check with their various websites.

One of these, the 'Maori Ranger Security Division', is a separate organisation ("we are not part of *Nu Tireni* Maori Government, *Te Wakaminenga* Maori Government or National *Wakaminenga*), although their website sets down a similar range of 'information', including an interview in which "Dr. Manuka Henare explains the 1835 *He Whakaputanga* and how Maori Sovereignty was NEVER ceded".[276] As the title suggests, this includes a policing unit.

The suggestion is put forward that many diverse groups can proceed independently to self-governance. "We do not need permission to activate or action our inherent customary rights provided we are acting in accordance to *tikanga*. ... The international indigenous and

---

[275] https://www.youtube.com/watch?v=9esAjPQOqZ8andab_channel=CWT
[276] https://www.maorirangersecuritydivision.com/home

native laws and imperial laws have already been set in place for our protection. In 2004 the United Nations Safety and Security Services recognised *Wakaminenga O Nga Hapu* as the autonomous native authority."

They claim that "The power is with *hapu* authority not *iwi*" and "encourage all *hapu* members nationwide to activate your *Wakaminenga O Nga Hapu* so you can enjoy the benefits of autonomy. Autonomy is when you are separate from your government. It is more a mental state of mind first .... then you will learn how to action your autonomy".[277]

Here is tribalism gone mad: not a separate Maori government, not many separate *iwi* entities, but a multiplicity of different *hapu* authorities.

They advertise "*Te-moana-nui-a-kiwa* Diplomatic Immunity Sea Pass Identity Cards" ($50 Adults and $25 Kids 18 and under), "in order to create a safe space for people to start activating their inherent customary rights and common law rights.[278] This appears to be claimed to be an international document, to provide 'diplomatic immunity' and to be "issued in accordance with the S2 Passports Act 1992".

Another anti-government group, reported by the 'Sovereign Citizen Movement' is the formation of 'Common law sheriffs', which believe that: "The common law is the law of God written by Him on the conscience of every man. It is the sacred duty of every freeborn man to defend that law and his own liberty before and over every obligation, yea even obligation to the state or to the King" (Sir Edward Coke, 1628).[279] This definition is similar to that given previously, and there are reports of a number of people offering these 'common law' courses.

---

[277] https://www.maorirangersecuritydivision.com/what-is-a-wakaminenga
[278] https://www.maorirangersecuritydivision.com/purchase-a-card
[279] https://commonlaw.earth/sheriffs/

These concepts destroy any understanding of and belief in the legitimacy of real common law, as taught in universities and generally understood. The resulting confusion creates conditions for the formation of destructive alternative power structures.

This lack of clarity has opened the way for more disputes. For example, in mid-2022, an argument between Ngai Tahu and the New Zealand Maori Council about how Maori representatives are to be selected is before the Waitangi Tribunal.[280] This concerns Resource Management Act changes where planning laws will be taken from local councils and given to 14 co-governed entities. Maori society has never been united, and is fundamentally divided today. Who is to hold this new power – *hapu*, *iwi*, federation or council?

An alternative government, destroying the unity of the nation, has been set up, and is unchallenged. Indeed, a fragmentation, a multiplicity of further alternative governments, is suggested. Unfortunately, these actions sit comfortably with the government policy of racial separation and co-governance. Such treasonable acts undermine the integrity, legitimacy and strength of the democratically elected parliament. The resultant confusion and disunity will reduce the real, and only, government's ability to get things done for the good of all New Zealanders.

---

[280] As reported in the New Zealand Herald

Apartheid in practice

New Zealand is now, in 2022, an apartheid state. We are divided into two separate races, with different rights and different facilities and organisations, by legislation – by definition and through a multiplicity of laws and practices. The country is well advanced towards the ultimate goal for 2040 set down clearly in *He Puapua*.

We have noted above some of the many reasons why we should be thankful and proud to be New Zealanders. We have noted the building of a nation using Western know-how, knowledge and expertise, so much to celebrate including major events as the nation was formed.

We have then seen with dismay how that structure has been unravelled, pulled apart. A people who joined with the intention of building a nation of one people (as stated clearly in article three of the Treaty where all New Zealanders became equal British citizens) have divided themselves. Previous champions of freedom and equality have been busy spreading division and constructing apartheid.

This is a strange story from the first, with the lost Treaty and unquestioning acceptance of the false version, to the recent rewriting of the Treaty to suit a separatist political agenda – so that now division is based on a treaty that initially made all citizens equal. There is much foolishness in the breakup of our nation. Perhaps the time has come for a dose of common sense, to seek clarity and to recognise what is happening.

I was once told that there was an unbridgeable gulf between people of different cultures. The suggestion was that neither I, nor anyone with ancestors who immigrated here after 1769, could possibly understand the early nineteenth century Maori or, indeed, the Maori of today. I ignored that direction and found, unsurprisingly, that

Maori are people just like myself, growing up with beliefs that came to be questioned, reacting and adjusting to changing circumstances. I soon came to respect many outstanding thinkers – including Hongi Hika, Tamati Waka Nene, Te Wherowhero, Tamihana Te Rauparaha, and later Apirana Ngata, James Carroll and Peter Buck. They, or their ancestors, came from a stone age culture but they had first class minds. When Television New Zealand chose to broadcast two reports suggesting that my books were "anti-Maori, hateful and untrue", it was evident that none had bothered to read the books they were attacking and attempting to ban.

Let us get to grips with what is happening here, now; to refuse to be confused by calls to ancient ways of *tikanga* and *matauranga*, which (we are told) we can never appreciate or comprehend. We must dare to ask, dare to think, dare to consider why such changes might be justified, what are the qualities that demand separate powers, and just what are the consequences of the new directions. Let us continue with self-confidence to ask what does all this mean in practice, taking nothing on trust and not being led astray by claims of a different way of thinking.

In the 'Three waters' proposal Maori are to have effective control, with half the authorities appointed by *iwi* and a water services regulator, *Taumata Arowai*, which will operate from a *te ao Maori* perspective. What is special about the pre-contact culture, and what additional understanding would Maori (chosen by race) bring to the development of modern sewage systems for cities?

Nothing; in traditional Maori society there was no treatment of effluent. As noted above, problems occurred in Wellington when an off-shore pipeline, satisfying the requirements of today's science, was blocked by a Maori refusal to accept any sewage in the sea.

There is now a separate Maori Health Authority guided by the old Maori culture – "developing the locality model of primary and community care in certain areas, some of which will take an approach centred on *kaupapa* Maori care" and "services grounded in *te ao*

Maori". This forgets the widespread concern with the state of Maori hygiene and the unsanitary conditions just over one hundred years ago, and the considerable opposition to traditional Maori healthcare practices by *tohunga*, leading to the celebration of the passing of the Tohunga Suppression Act in 1907.

So, too with law, which can now be directed by local *tikanga*, again ignoring the absence of any pre-contact system of law, as demonstrated by the many calls by Maori to 'give us law' and the appreciation of that gift by chiefs at Kohimarama in 1860 such as – "Under the old law we perished; under the present law we live" (Hemi Matini Te Nera), "In my opinion the greatest blessings are, Christianity and the Laws" (Hemi Metene Te Awaitaia), "It was the law of Christianity that put an end to our cannibal practices" (Tamihana Te Raupahara).[281] Law is no longer comprehensible to the ordinary citizen.

In education, there is a separate school system, with a very different curriculum; do not forget that pre-contact Maori were illiterate. This is to allow "the right of indigenous peoples to establish and control their own educational systems and institutions, including pre-school and university level". There is a general requirement to "integrate Maori history, culture, perspectives and languages into the national education curricula."

The freedom of the previously largely autonomous universities each governed by a professorial board has gone (as has the ability of scientists to control their own affairs with the death of the DSIR). A twelve-person board at each university now has a minority of university representatives: only two are from the professional staff; four are appointed by central government, one is the CEO (directing himself/herself), one person is an enrolled student, one is an alumnus of the university appointed by the Council, two are persons able to provide skills specified by the Council. The twelfth is a Maori, able

---

[281] Robinson 2022, pages 38 44, 45

to advise the Council on issues relevant to Maori, appointed by the Council following a call for expressions of interest from *iwi* and other Maori individuals or groups.[282] Again and again, Maori are treated differently with addition representation, yet with no realistic contribution from *tikanga*.

Otago University has a policy for research consultation with Maori. Any researcher (in any topic, in a wide range of subjects unknown to *tikanga*) is required to 'consult' so as to assure that their work satisfies "the needs and aspirations of Ngai Tahu for Maori development and benefit in Ngai Tahu Vision 2025".[283]

Waikato University places considerable emphasis on *tikanga*. "The world is looking to Indigenous knowledge to solve modern-day issues. Rated as one of the leading *Matauranga Maori* centres in the country, we represent innovation and tradition in teaching and research, and provide global leadership in sustainable development and Indigenous issues."[284]

So too with Canterbury University. "The University of Canterbury has announced five new professor positions and the introduction of a new treaty partnership office, building on its commitment to strengthen Maori leadership and relationships. *Ka Waimaero* (the *Ngai Tahu* Research Centre) will be the foundation for the new office of treaty partnership, believed to be the first of its kind among Aotearoa universities to embed *mana whenua – Te Runanga o Ngai Tahu* – into the structure of *Te Whare Wananga o Waitaha* University of Canterbury."[285]

---

[282] https://www.auckland.ac.nz/en/about-us/about-the-university/the-university/governance-and-committees/university-council/appointments-to-the-university-of-auckland-council.html
[283] https://www.otago.ac.nz/research/maoriconsultation/
[284] https://www.waikato.ac.nz/study/campaigns/maori-and-indigenous-studies
[285] https://www.stuff.co.nz/pou-tiaki/126463329/university-of-canterbury-now-new-zealands-first-treaty-university

This is just part of the story. There is the indigenous peoples scam, with the picture of wrongful colonisation that is the very opposite of what really happened; the construction of an absurd, long list of wrongs by the permanent Waitangi Tribunal; the requirement for separate, unequal Maori representation in both arms of government and in organisations across the country; the never-ending provision of money and powers to *iwi* through Treaty settlements, based on a newly minted version of the treaty; the rewriting of the Foreshore and Seabed legislation to please a litigant minority. Many people have become angered at the insistence of the use of a Maori language, which is understood by few, and the renaming of our country as *Aotearoa* while refusing a referendum on it, just as *He Puapua* is being followed despite being absent in the last election and hidden since. So much is carried out by stealth, not placed before the public, not open to scrutiny – and so much effort is put into silencing those who ask questions and speak out.

Previous chapters have outlined some of the many occasions to celebrate in New Zealand history, and have recognised the efforts of so many to build a modern and prosperous nation. This chapter has pointed out the nonsense of many actions to divide us and set *tikanga* as a guide and control for many activities, when it was the overturn of much of *tikanga* that opened the way to a considerable improvement in Maori life. It is silly, and ineffective, and it should be set aside.

If this is nonsense, then why is it succeeding? This is not held as a political ideology by either of the main parties, both of which have in the past stood against racism. Yet both the previous Key government and the current Ardern government have acted to bring in divisive legislation – in order to gain the support of the Maori Party and other MPs from Maori seats (which should have been gone long ago, and which would go if there was a referendum).

The process only provides for the greed of the powerful Maori elite, who have built up an impressive and powerful array of networks, who have profited considerably and will continue to prosper. The country has lost its way, and lost a sense of unity and togetherness, has lost equality, and democracy has been undermined.

PART 4: RECOVERY

The good life: equality and democracy

No, Monsieur le Comte, you shan't have her! You shan't have her. Because you are a great noble, you think you are a great genius! Nobility, a fortune, a rank, appointments to office: all this makes a man so proud! What did you do to earn all this? **You took the trouble to get born – nothing more.** *Moreover, you're really a pretty ordinary fellow. While as for me, lost in the crowd, I've had to use more knowledge, more brains, just to keep alive than your likes have to spend on governing Spain and the Empire for a century.*
The barber scorns the Count, in *The marriage of Figaro*, Pierre Beaumarchais, 1778, which was made into an opera by Wolfgang Amadeus Mozart in 1786.

Above all we want equal political rights. I know this sounds revolutionary to the whites of the country because the majority of the voters will be Africans. This makes the white man fear democracy. But this fear cannot be allowed to stand in the way of the only solution which will guarantee racial harmony and freedom for all.
Nelson Mandela 1964: from the dock at the Rivonia trial, when accused with three counts of sabotage.

We hold these truths to be self-evident, that all men are created equal
American Declaration of Independence, 1776
Quoted by Martin Luther King in the March on Washington for Jobs and Freedom on August 28, 1963, calling for an end to racism

All human beings are born free and equal in dignity and rights.
United Nations Universal Declaration of Human Rights 1948

A call for equality echoes through the years, recognised as a basic condition for the conquest of racism. The opposite, of privilege based on race, leads to oppression. This is our heritage; this is our culture; this is who we are – across the political spectrum, setting the ground rules for debate and disagreement, compromise where possible. But there must be no compromise on that basic condition.

New Zealand has a proud history of bringing and extending equality: all New Zealanders were given British citizenship (without distinction, with no separation or partnership; Article 3 of the Treaty is clear on this) in 1840 when the nation was formed, and slaves were set free; in 1879, the right to vote was extended to all men, regardless of whether they owned or rented property; in 1893, New Zealand became the first self-governing country in the world in which women had the right to vote in parliamentary elections; in 1986, members of the gay community gained equal rights.

That last was the outcome of a long and courageous fight by a Cabinet Minister in the Labour government, Fran Wilde. In 1985 she introduced the Homosexual Law Reform Bill, sparking 16 months of heated debate. Wilde became the target of hate mail and death threats, as well as tirades from critics in the Opposition. When the Bill was passed, a member of the public pointed at Wilde amid the cheers and pronounced God's curse on her. This is the dark side of New Zealand: efforts to impose one religion and dogma on others, which is particularly blatant in today's divided nation.

As with a number of contentious issues, those opposed may hold their particular views and base their private actions on their beliefs; what is important here is that we are free, with equal rights, to run our private lives as we choose.

Many Maori, like the count in *The marriage of Figaro*, claim special rights only because they "took the trouble to get born – nothing more"; they claim that since they have some ancestors whom they label 'indigenous', they are special. No, we are born equal and must live equal.

The idea of 'a fair go' was once thought basic to the New Zealand character, with many steps taken to move ever closer to the ideal of equality, to settle disputes (and even war) and learn to become one people of equals. But, since the formation of the Waitangi Tribunal, 47 years ago in 1975, there have been a series of increasingly drastic steps backwards, to inequality, institutional racism and apartheid.

There was once, from the very inception of this nation, a desire to be one people, to move towards greater unity through the years.

He iwi tahi tatou – now we are equal
Lieutenant-Governor William Hobson at Waitangi, February 5, 1840

I say, people of Ngatitoa, of Whanganui, and of Ngatiwhakaue, you must tie us into a bundle that we may rest on the law, both soul and body. ... Let the Governor tie us in a bundle. He understands what measures to devise for us. Let us leave it to Waka Nene also to tie us in a bundle, for he is resting on the (Governor's) system. Let the Government also tie us in a bundle.
Wiremu Nero Te Awaitaia at Kohimarama, 1860[286]

Both British and Maori early expressed a desire to be governed as one, and to become ever more a united people. Current New Zealand leadership appears, <u>at first sight</u>, to say the same.

We are one
Jacinda Ardern at Christchurch, March 2019

---

[286] Robinson 2022, page 114

But sadly, Ardern is two-faced. That seeming accord with Hobson is undermined, indeed contradicted, as her government continues its plans for extensive co-governance with a comprehensive separation by race into two distinct groups with different rights and powers (following in the footsteps of the previous John Key government with their recognition of the divisive United Nations Declaration on the Rights of Indigenous People).

That previous ideal of unity is explicitly opposed by Maori activists, such as Maori Party co-leader Rawiri Waititi, who wants a *tiriti*-centric *Aotearoa* where "the majority doesn't rule over Maori, **not a democracy** – we want to be in total control of our sovereignty. ... Waititi doesn't think an Upper House for *tangata whenua* goes far enough. He wants a completely independent Maori Parliament."[287]

Here is an unequivocal refusal to accept the Treaty signed by Maori in 1840, where the first article was that "The chiefs of the Confederation of the United Tribes and the other chiefs who have not joined the confederation cede to the Queen of England for ever the entire Sovereignty of their country." Here is a complete turn away from the ideals on which this nation was formed. Where are the shouts of anger? Is anyone awake out there?

Some Maori are so focussed on themselves that they forget that there are other people living in this country. We must make our voices heard and stop allowing ourselves to be pushed aside like this.

Once I felt that this land is our land – this land belongs to you and me, all of us.[288] As a student (1961), I hitchhiked from Auckland and walked up through the National Park to the Ketetahi hot springs high on the slopes of Mount Tongariro, where I heated my meal and had a hot bath, while looking out across the snow-covered slopes. After

---

[287] https://www.newshub.co.nz/home/politics/2021/07/not-in-a-democracy-m-ori-party-co-leader-rawiri-waititi-outlines-his-vision-for-a-tiriti-centric-aotearoa-where-the-majority-doesn-t-rule-over-m-ori.html
[288] Woody Guthrie 1940, "This land is your land", song

a freezing night, comfortable in my warm sleeping bag, gazing upwards at sparkling stars, I repeated the meal and bath before walking across the tinkling snow crystals to a hut and then on to the Chateau – a magical couple of days. Now it has been decided that the springs are on private Maori land: they are fenced off, no longer freely open.

This is the picture across the country. In 2010 a proposal by Treaty Minister Finlayson to hand Urewera National Park to Tuhoe was strongly criticised and rejected at a National Party regional conference. But soon after, Prime Minister Key went ahead and ignored the opinions of party members; the park was given away.[289]

As just one of many further examples, Punakaiki once belonged to us all, administered by the Department of Conservation (DOC). Now a commercial $26 million Punakaiki visitor centre, jointly funded by DOC and the Provincial Growth Fund, will be gifted to Poutini Ngai Tahu on completion and DOC will lease (pay for) space in it for its visitor services. Three members of the West Coast Conservation Board have resigned saying they have been called racist for raising what they see as conflicts between the interests of conservation and the interests of Ngai Tahu.[290] This is the reality of co-management and working in partnership.

I am a New Zealander; I belong here, nowhere else. But that sense of belonging, that this is our country, has gone. We want belonging: this is high on lists of fundamental human needs – for all the diversity amongst the human family, there are some basic features which we share. An examination of human needs suggests that in an ideal society everybody should be given the opportunity to be a part of the social fabric, to belong.[291] But once a special position is given to one group, all others are set aside as second-class citizens.

---

[289] Barr et al 2015, page 218
[290] *Otago Daily Times*, Saturday, 2 July 2022
[291] Robinson 2013, pages 23-24

This has meaning for today's New Zealand, where it should be that fellowship to all is of greater worth than indigenous ancestry, and a simple belief in equality of greater value than Maori blood.

All of this, equality and belonging, demand the unity of a real democracy, where all electors have the same rights, deciding on both local and central government together with each vote having the same value. This is not the way in current New Zealand, where there are separate wards and seats, of different price, coupled with different rights in law (as well as sudden reversals of policy, by both major parties, and key agenda kept hidden during elections). Rather than moving towards greater unity and equality, these differences have been increased, and entrenched in law.

"The *He Puapua* Report proposes revolutionary change for New Zealand. The question of how we have arrived at a crossroads where New Zealanders will have to choose between an ethno-nationalist state – which *He Puapua* leads to – or a democratic-nationalist one has its origins in three events in 1985, 1986 and 1987." Elisabeth Rata has followed those developments, with a particular reference to a return to division into separate *iwi*. "Tribalism and democracy are incompatible – they cannot exist together as political systems in one nation. The condition for democracy is everywhere the end of tribalism with its birth-ascribed inequality and exclusive kin membership."[292]

A common belief in equality in politics, and a real democratic system, was once held by all New Zealanders, across the political spectrum. Behind political differences and disagreements over particular policies lay a shared commitment. Recently, the destruction of democracy and the division of people has been by both major parties and several minor ones. This is no time for empty finger-pointing or exaggerated claims; the need is for all concerned New Zealanders to work together – to have the courage to speak out and be ready to

---

[292] Rata 2021, Robinson, pages 3, 17-19

support others despite deeply-felt divergence on other topics, and to take on racism by refusing to accept that label when that smear is broadcast by those who bring apartheid to our society. Then we can recover our country, which has so sadly lost all sense of balance, so that:

1. all citizens of New Zealand have the same political rights and duties,

2. all political authority comes from the people by democratic means including, always, a united ballot of all the electorate together, noting that

3. New Zealand is a multi-ethnic liberal democracy where discrimination based on ethnicity is illegal.

The great challenge ahead

There are many powerful organisations, national and local *iwi*, pushing for division and for special rights based on race. This point has been made previously, and must be repeated here:

"This revolution is being carried out by an array of co-operating organisations. There are many *hapu* and *iwi* groups across the country. There is the Maori king movement which started in the Waikato in 1858 and then led a rebellion[293], the Maori Council set up in 1962, the 1987 *Iwi* Leaders' Forum[294], now the *Iwi* Chairs Forum first convened in 2005[295], the political Maori Party and the powerful Maori caucus in the Labour Party.

Those groups have considerable power and have been effective within government. Jacinda Ardern is a puppet, a front for Nanaia Mahuta (who has strong links to the king movement). Separatists have been active in formulating major policy initiatives."

Planning for separation has been ongoing for many decades, and many of those activities have been very successful, such as the approaches to the United Nations resulting in reports calling for changes to New Zealand law, the signing of the United Nations Declaration on the Rights of Indigenous People, and the current writing of divisive policies set down in the *He Puapua* report.

They are very well funded. The continuing Treaty settlements had reached $3,554 million by 2018.[296] Many are well paid for government positions while supporting their endeavours for Maori rights and *tikanga* over universal rights and a common culture. A considerable number of organisations provide positions and

---

[293] Robinson 2016
[294] Rata 2021
[295] Robinson 2022, pages 58-59
[296] Robinson et al 2013 and 2018, page 47 of appendix

payments; the beneficiaries will be aggrieved if their jobs go and will fight hard to protect their livelihood. Since such jobs are given on the basis of race, their removal will be seen as 'anti-Maori'.

These many groups have repeated stories of wrongs of the past, and built a considerable set of beliefs, demanding that recompense is due. In doing so the considerable efforts to build a fair society are swept aside, ignored; the construction of a worldview and a dogma has been separate, not inclusive of other New Zealanders, and not open to question and debate. This has become the equivalent of an extreme, fundamentalist, religious sect. They will fight for their position; they are determined and convinced. Reasoned argument will not win the day; this is about propaganda and power.

This is ideology, not reason; entitlement, not equality and fair play. We must tell the pigs that they can no longer rule the farmyard (*Animal Farm*), the count that he cannot have his way with Susanna (*The Marriage of Figaro*). Apartheid must be put an end to, without compromise of principle.

Their position is strong. There have been no significant challenges to the Maori seats, to the rewriting of history by the Waitangi Tribunal, or to the continuing handing over of public moneys through Treaty settlements based on insufficient, or non-existent, grounds of supposed wrongs. That belief in terrible wrongs by colonisation, the very opposite of the real story, has become an accepted dogma for the nation.

A whole generation has been brought up to believe that there are two very different treaties, the 'English Treaty' and *Te Tiriti o Waitangi*. There is an insistence on partnership rather than unity of one people, and racism has reversed its meaning – to argue against racism and the race-defined Maori special rights (as 'indigenous *tangata whenua'*) is falsely called 'racism'. It is widely thought that Don Brash is a racist since he called for equality – in opposition to true racism – in his speech at Orewa in 2004.[297]

Recent generations have been conditioned (and their beliefs have been influenced) by the repetition of exaggerated and often untrue stories of terrible past wrongs (including imagined happenings at Parihaka and Rangiaowhia), while the horrors of the pre-Treaty tribal wars and of the massacres committed by Maori rebels are forgotten. The messages of Part One here (how New Zealanders came together and many Maori celebrated colonisation) and Part Two (how people from across the world built this nation) are missing.

Education curricula are proposed calling for Maori to be proud to be Maori (not New Zealanders) while others are asked to feel shame. The United Nations rapporteurs have been fed such biased accounts, which they simply believed in their ignorance, and they have written reports asking for a full acceptance of separatist political demands. The constant repetition of these stories, supported by the compliant media, has created a general belief of past wrongs that fuels the acceptance of Maori exceptionalism as 'indigenous' people deserving of special and different rights.

It is a tough task, to put right these decades of conditioning.

The major bulwark against this tsunami of separatism, so graphically described in *He Puapua*, would seem to lie in politics, to vote for political parties that support equality. Once they gain influence and control of the all-powerful parliament, laws can be passed to overturn division and set the country back on track.

But we know that we cannot trust politicians. The two glaring recent examples are those of National under John Key, with the radical rewrite of the Foreshore and Seabed legislation and the signing of the United Nations Declaration on the Rights of Indigenous Peoples, and Labour under Jacinda Ardern who accepted the rewritten Foreshore

---

[297] https://www.scoop.co.nz/stories/PA0401/S00220.htm

and Seabed legislation and the UNDRIP declaration (thus reversing the previous Labour Party policy) and kept secret the revolutionary *He Puapua* proposals (not mentioned in the election campaign) while acting to carry out its wishes.

It would be foolish indeed to put too much faith in that one path as we fight for recovery of a unified country, free of the racism of a chosen people. Any successful politician will first consider how to gain power, which is all too often by following the accepted dogma of the day and not by voicing a potentially unpopular observation that the emperor has no clothes: "Courage is the rarest of all qualities to be found in public men."[298]

Politicians, of many political parties, have shown themselves to be devious and untrustworthy. All too often, decisions are reached without any understanding. As noted above, a previous Treaty Minister Doug Graham made it clear that this lack of clarity was purposeful and that Parliament had handed over the task of writing law to the courts.

That has been disastrous, as judges have seized the opportunity to invent even more confused law. While there is a need to work with, and face up to, the political establishment, only a fool would place any trust in the judiciary. The courts must be brought under control by the writing, and passing, of clear law that allows no room for manoeuvre and that removes the double standards for New Zealanders of Maori and other ethnicities.

All too often, those in power, directing the affairs of the nation, show that they simply don't know what they are doing. The incompetence that has become a feature of New Zealand was shown clearly with the launch of the Maori Health Authority. Here again is the claim that: "Our health and disability system has underperformed for Maori

---

[298] attributed to Benjamin Disraeli (1804-1881).

for too long – life expectancy is seven years less than for *pakeha*".[299] As pointed out above the facts show clearly that the difference had reduced considerably under the previous, successful system, and the remaining gap is a likely consequence of the move after 1984 from a mixed economy to liberalisation and free trade. A solution would come from understanding and tackling the real problem.

They have no clear idea of how to proceed and of what changes will bring better results, just racial separation and a new bureaucracy. "These reforms are designed to give Maori *rangatiratanga* over *hauora Maori* and greater influence throughout the system. This is not only because it is central to *Te Tiriti o Waitangi*, but also to ensure everyone has the same access to good health outcomes."[300] But just what are the proposed actions to improve health? Certainly, traditional Maori health is not the way to go; the Maori life expectancy was so much lower then, around 20-25 years before the country was formed. **Separate government is their aim, not better healthcare and a more efficient system.**

New Zealand has been overwhelmed by a determined minority, who have constructed a comprehensive plan of action (so clear in *He Puapua*) and are building towards a completely separated and racially defined government system. Their effort needs to be matched and overcome, by an equally vigorous effort.

Togetherness and *aroha* (concern and respect for others) are absent; it is not just public figures (mud thrown at Brash, Clark reduced to tears at Waitangi) who have been attacked – many of us have felt the aggression and suffered from abuse. It will take years, a generation, to turn back the tide and recover from this tsunami, to return to a country with a fair go for all, and mutual respect. There is a big job to be done.

---

[299] https://dpmc.govt.nz/sites/default/files/2021-04/htu-factsheet-hauora-maori-en-apr21.pdf
[300] op cit

Major policies

He Puapua promised, and is delivering, a deluge of changes, a political and cultural revolution. This apartheid must be turned back with an equal, and equally decisive, counter-revolution. Not little by little, but a complete and determined assertion of equality and fair play, a firm reassertion of democracy.

This is not the divisiveness of the main body of the UNDRIP report but a celebration of the equality demanded by the clear statement of principle with which it is introduced, insisting (inter alia) that all policies advocating superiority of peoples on the basis of racial or ethnic differences are racist, morally condemnable and socially unjust. Here is the basic principle that must guide the nation.

- All New Zealanders are born equal. There can be no differentiation in public affairs (central and local government, public organisations and law) based on of inheritance, race or ethnicity. Such racism is unacceptable to the nation.

A number of definite actions must be taken to remove race-based differentiation from the laws of New Zealand. These must be firm and definitive, prompt and comprehensive, with the repeal of **all** race-based legislation.

- Close the Waitangi Tribunal, immediately.

- Remove the Treaty of Waitangi from all law and statutes; the original document has been reinterpreted completely, to become very different from the original, and remains only as a subject of discord.

- End Treaty settlements; this may be followed by a process of public hearings and vigorous promotion of public interests, true hearings presenting a full depiction of the past, rather than a one-sided sham.

- Withdraw from the 2001 United Nations Commission on Human Rights resolution and the 2007 United Nations Declaration on the Rights of Indigenous Peoples, both of which permit United Nations agencies to act as a court of appeal, and have allowed ill-informed rapporteurs to make pronouncements on the laws and government of New Zealand, which is outside the bounds of the United Nations.

- Repeal the Marine and Coastal Area Act 2011, and reinstate the Clark government's Foreshore and Seabed Act 2004.

- Move to abolish separate Maori wards (local government) and seats (national government), with a binding nationwide poll.

- The name of this country is New Zealand. (The Maori Party has a petition to Parliament to change the name to *Aotearoa*[301] without any involvement of other New Zealanders.) There must be no thought of a change of name without a binding nationwide poll.

- Repeal the Three Waters proposal, and assert the status quo *ante*.

- Scrap the Maori Health Authority and reassert one common, universal health system for all New Zealanders.

- Rescind the rewritten education curriculum and re-assert the status quo *ante*.

- Remove all reference to *tikanga* in law and regulations. Belief systems such as Christianity and *tikanga* have no place in the

---

[301] https://www.parliament.nz/en/pb/petitions/document/PET_124093/petition-of-te-p%C4%81ti-m%C4%81ori-change-our-official-name-to

governance of a multi-cultural and multi-ethnic society in the twenty-first century.

This is a partial list, setting the framework for a comprehensive revisit to a wide range of divisive legislation (one example is the Canterbury Regional Council (Ngai Tahu Representation) Bill). A number of supporting actions are called for.

- Clarify and explain the need for separation of the judicial and legislative branches of government. Rewrite law to provide clear guidance to judges, who no longer will have the power to interpret vague prescriptions and thus effectively to determine the law.

- New Zealand lacks any appreciation of constitutional understanding. An effort must be made to expand the political and educational knowledge of philosophy and principles basic to good government (provided suitable scholars can be found; the discussions on constitutional issues led by Geoffrey Palmer were lacking in clarity and understanding).

Such ideas are not new; a "Principles of the Treaty of Waitangi Deletion Bill" was introduced by Doug Woolerton (New Zealand First party) with a first reading in July 2006 and a second reading in November 2007, when it failed.[302] More recently, Elisabeth Rata has provided a thoughtful analysis of the current situation: "It's a coup d'état in all but name, accomplished not by force but by ideology – enabled by a compliant media.". Her choice of a set of actions to put things right starts with the essential call to: "Remove the treaty and its principles from all legislation."[303]

New Zealand's unicameral parliament is rare among developed nations – even individual states in federal systems most often have two houses, providing a check on the otherwise unbridled power of

---

[302] Robinson 2011, Appendix 3, pages 101-102
[303] Rata 2022

one chamber, which here is largely in the hands of a few who dominate the Cabinet. The drift to racism might have been checked by action in an independent upper house.

However, we should leave aside the idea of an upper house for now, as there is a great danger from the idea of a racially divided House. Current ideas include a racial division of an upper house into two race-based parts, each with decisive power, making racism a core feature of the nation. The danger is too great, and we must put the idea aside for now.

We should similarly resist any calls for a written constitution, for two reasons. Firstly, that, with the current climate, it would likely be racially divisive. Secondly, that it would, like the constitution of the USA, be open to various interpretations (just as the Treaty of Waitangi has been, a political football), thus handing political power to the unelected Supreme Court (itself appointed by government).

Combined action

New Zealand is being transformed by a comprehensive revolution, destroying a way of life and turning away from its founding principles. This ongoing revolution is well advanced towards its final goal of full-blooded apartheid, with domination of the narrative and the media, and increasing control of bodies of state; acceptance of co-governance and the final division of the country is well within sight.

All too often in New Zealand politics the direction of the country is defined by whoever holds the balance of power in Parliament – often the Maori Party, which has made much use of that controlling position.

Politicians have bowed down before this campaign; the Labour and National parties have been turned, to reverse their previous policies. Now, in 2022, Labour and the Green Party have become committed to the clearly proclaimed constitutional transformation.

One challenge for the people (depending on the individual political stance) is either to gain sufficient influence with a major party in order to force a definite commitment to equality, or to push for a similar commitment from a third party and give the preferred option sufficient support to attain that deciding position. But such action has proved inadequate in the past; there must be a much greater push towards equality.

A fight-back, a counter-revolution, is long overdue. More of the people of New Zealand must dare to speak out, to wake up and to face up to the powerful propaganda machine that has so much control over the media, to refuse to bow down to pressure, with each doing whatever we can. **You don't win an argument with silence.**

This will involve a variety of actions, by individuals and groups, both within the political system and within society at large. The Maori separatist movement has been active for many decades and has considerable organisational strength. This will be a long struggle, demanding a similar determination, a countervailing organisation. Let us hope that many Maori can come to recognise the true benefits of the development of New Zealand and the value of equality, so that this can be a fight for principle and not a struggle between opposing races – as has been forced by the Maori elite. We must aspire to become one people once more.

Exit or voice

Members of any organisation, whether a business, a nation or any other form of human grouping, have a choice to make when they perceive that the organisation is demonstrating a decrease in quality or benefit to the members.

There are three options open to dissatisfied citizens: *exit, voice or loyalty*. They can leave the country, emigrate. They can be active, protest and try to encourage those responsible to put things right. Or they can simply do nothing, preferring for one reason or another to 'suffer in silence'.[304]

With too great a choice of exit or loyalty (to emigrate or do nothing), a system, be it business or political, may collapse. This is the situation now in New Zealand as so many have chosen to sit aside, as equality has gone, democracy is crumbling, and apartheid is becoming established. All too many have chosen to remain ignorant and to walk away (or grumble to themselves) as racial differences are extended. The situation has become critical, and more need to take part by the choice of the voice option – to become active.

A greater fight-back is long overdue. This must be a powerful citizens' effort, a people's counter-revolution, involving the formation of both local and co-operating national groups, gathering and spreading information through talks and group 'teach-ins'

---

[304] Hirschman, 1970, page 78; Robinson 1989, pages 77-78

(extending efforts that have been under way for some time, but not yet adequate to the task).

Most of us are pretty ordinary, nonaggressive. It is difficult to stand up, and speak out, against the bullying and abuse of the new racists (this is no exaggeration, many have suffered verbal attacks, bordering on the physical, and many have been scared off). Supportive groups can assist a new assertiveness.

One recent small victory has been the success of demonstrations against a proposal to bring co-governance to Rotorua – for three Maori ward seats, three general ward seats, and four at-large seats. That arrangement would have split the people into race-defined groups, and give the 19,791 citizens on the Maori roll 2.6 times the voting power of the 51,618 citizens on the general roll. Demonstrators pointed out that the council was "blatantly ignoring the overwhelming message from ratepayers that they do not accept race-based decisions", and that "co-governance is basically the antithesis of democracy... the minority ruling over the majority."[305] The Attorney-General, David Parker, was forced to recognise that the Rotorua proposal was in breach of the Bill of Rights Act and was discriminatory; it was withdrawn, and the Maori Affairs Committee halted hearings of scheduled oral submissions.

It would be foolish to believe that such fights are over; the juggernaut rolls on, as with Three Waters, the Maori Health Authority, and much more. As two examples among many: (1) the Department of Conservation is calling on *iwi* across the country to help the agency better manage visitors and run New Zealand's nature, culture and heritage sites. But this is our land; we all care, and Maori *tikanga* has shown no particular capacity for environmental concern (think of the moa, so quickly driven to extinction). (2) On August 3, 2002, the Canterbury Regional Council (Ngai Tahu Representation) Bill

---

[305]

https://www.democracyaction.org.nz/rotorua_lakes_council_pushing_for_maori_co_governance

passed its final reading giving Ngai Tahu two unelected seats on the Canterbury Regional Council.

We certainly do not want the constitutional transformation that is planned for New Zealand, and now openly spoken of. How many understand what is meant? Meanwhile, the Maori Party has been openly celebrating the success of their constitutional transformation. That will be so, unless a sufficient force gathers and turns it back.

The way to win is to be daring, to force the issue and make clear and well-supported demands. First and most important is to move decisively back to a belief in one people of equals, no longer split by race into Maori and the other.

Established groups

Action can be readily taken to expand the existing anti-racism movement, to join and support one of the several groups that argue for the desired equality and unity. These include Hobson's Pledge, 1Law4All, the Taxpayer's Union, Democracy Action and the New Zealand Centre for Political Research.

In 2022, just one political party with MPs in parliament has established itself in a call for equality: the ACT Party position is clear. NZ First has argued against the division of the country but has been unable to make much ground and its future is currently uncertain.

This is in any case not a party-specific issue: many from across all parts of the political spectrum, from far right to far left, support the principles of equality which have been proclaimed by so many leaders, from Tom Paine to Thomas Jefferson, and accepted (in principle) by the diverse members of the United Nations.

Those groups have done a great deal, organised talks and petitions, provided information and distributed leaflets[306]. There have been some successes, such as the (temporary) halt to co-governance in Rotorua noted above.

A vigorous campaign temporarily held up the Three Waters project, and delivered 68,661 submissions by 65,091 New Zealanders opposing that legislation[307], but the government went ahead. The revised Bill removed one of the claimed reasons for the change, the raising of finance using ownership of public resources as security, being "able to borrow against the assets to build new infrastructure". The Bill, in August, 2022, stated that "an entity must not use water services assets as security for any purpose".

Since there had been criticism over ownership, the revised Bill claimed the assets remained in council ownership – while within the Bill it is stated that "water services assets are owned and operated by a water services entity". The Taxpayer's Union sought legal advice on this contradiction. "The legal opinion is very detailed, but it is not hard to understand. It calls the claims of retention of local ownership 'false, misleading and deceptive' as 'councils are expressly denied the rights of possession, control, derivation of benefits, and disposition that are the defining attributes of ownership'. Gary Judd QC comments in his review of the legal opinion: 'When all the lying statements are put together, as [the] opinion does, the government's effrontery is breath-taking'."[308]

All have experienced problems with the biased media and captured authorities, which act to block free speech and the spread of information. The Coastal Coalition and NZCPR Citizens' Initiated

---

[306] such as: 1Law4All, *Are we being conned by the treaty industry*, http://1law4all.kiwi.nz/treaty-industry-con/
[307] Taxpayers Union, 'Stop Three Waters Roadshow'
[308] Taxpayers Union August 2022, *Legal Opinion: Three Waters Bill "Calculated To Deceive"*, https://www.scoop.co.nz/stories/PO2208/S00017/legal-opinion-three-waters-bill-calculated-to-deceive.htm

Referendum, asking that the 2011 Marine and Coastal Area Act be replaced by legislation that restores Crown ownership of the foreshore and seabed[309], came under savage attack by the attorney-general Christopher Finlayson, who called them 'clowns' and 'profoundly sickening'; the referendum failed to attain the requisite number of signatures.

These efforts face significant opposition. For example, in July, 2022, the Taxpayer's Union (spokesman Peter Williams) was banned from the Local Government New Zealand conference on 'the future of local government'; the justification was that "the Taxpayers' Union has previously criticised LGNZ", with the President of LGNZ saying that they are not welcome because "we don't trust what you might say" about the event. This argument for silencing a critic is patently ludicrous; it is, however, the New Zealand of today.

The reality is that these worthy groups are struggling to gain the attention of the wider public, and to thus attain a sufficient membership to swing the debate, to change public perceptions and to gain meaningful power. Much more is required.

Combining; an umbrella group

There is one obvious limitation: each of these groups has a philosophical stance additional to a belief in the principle of equality. This is uncomfortable to those of other persuasions, and limits the potential membership.

The door must be open for a diversity of viewpoints; there is a need for a 'wider church', an umbrella organisation to be inclusive of all political groups, with only one clear goal, which is an insistence on equality in law and government, and a refusal of racial separation. Such a grouping must be comfortable for people from all political beliefs, aiming to form an equal society no matter what political ideology is dominant. Then I, despite my philosophical differences

---

[309] https://www.nzcpr.com/test-post-578/

with all of these groups, could join in whole-heartedly, and there would be a much greater potential membership for a citizen's counter-revolution to reverse the *He Puapua* tsunami.

This must be a meeting-place for New Zealanders of many political persuasions, free of partisanship. Many of the left and the right have a strong belief in equality, and this racism sits outside that political spectrum. Thus far, the right has been most vocal, and an inclusive grouping will provide an opportunity for left-wing thinkers to also play a more active part.

The goal must be simple, unambiguous and direct. **Just equality.**

A nationwide co-ordinating and networking structure is called for, possibly a small team, financed by a combination of big donors and personal contributions. This would help in the assembling and distribution of information, and the gathering of signatures, as well as for the development of co-ordination among the participating groups.

Force the issue and open up the debate

Recent policies set down by a determined minority are tearing the country apart. Most New Zealanders are ignorant, and are kept ignorant by government actions, aided by media bias and silence. The dice are loaded and free speech is limited.

The pressing need is to open the box and get it all out, to understand the harm that has been done, is being done, and will be done. And to gather in sufficient numbers to turn this monster around, to defeat the destructive revolution with its push towards apartheid, co-governance.

The way to move decisively forward is to focus on one clear issue to blow open the debate and break through media silence; just **equality**. This must be followed by an action to catch the attention of the country and provide a rallying point to bring together the diverse groups opposed to inequality, to provide a ready (**and widely**

acceptable) cause for those who have been holding back. A new co-ordinating group must be formed (building on existing organisations, with an open door for others to join in) and a choice made of the preferred unified action. It is essential to generate sufficient numbers to display a groundswell of opinion that must be taken seriously.

There are a number of actions possible for this, including a citizen's initiated referendum, a petition to Parliament, a road show moving across the country, a march on parliament, leaflet drops, letter-writing campaigns and group messages to local MPs pledging to refuse to vote for them unless they support equality. A simple message summarising the urgent need for action and introducing the project being put into action can be put online and publicised by all groups.

Discussions with colleagues have identified strengths and weaknesses of each of the actions noted. Indeed, many such efforts have been carried out by the organisations listed above, with varied success. It would be up to the umbrella groups to determine how best to proceed. **Most important is the decision to take effective and vigorous joint action.**

That first action is not an end in itself, rather a means to an end. The goal is to form a clear focus, now, for a national outcry, to contribute to consciousness-raising and to provide the basis for a nation-wide, co-operative organisation. This would be the first aim of the proposed unifying coalition.

This will, unfortunately, be the start of a long campaign. It has been 47 years since the beginning of the effort to split New Zealand, with the formation of the Waitangi Tribunal in 1975. That damage will not be repaired in one day and the crusade of the Maori elite to gain control will not be defeated without a struggle. It will take time and effort to bring all New Zealanders back together as one people.

It is hoped that the major themes of this book – a recognition that there is much in colonisation to celebrate and a realisation of the contributions that so many, diverse, people have made to the building of the nation – will come to the forefront as the debate breaks free from current restraints. We should all be proud of our heritage, proud to be New Zealanders.

Bibliography

Adcock F 2012. *The UN Special Rapporteur on the Rights of Indigenous Peoples and New Zealand: a study in compliance ritualism.* New Zealand Yearbook of International Law Vol 10, pages 97-120

Adkin G L 1952. *Geological Evidence of the Antiquity of Man in the NZ Area.* https://horowhenua.kete.net.nz/item/b2115abe-f93c-4c57-98b0-6da961dad4bb/pdf

Barr H and Robinson J L 2013. *Dialogue with the Race Relations Office on racism and the Treaty.* A copy is included at the end of a lengthy blog, racerelationsracism.blogspot.com

Barr H, Brash D, Butler M, Chapple R, Cresswell P, Moon B, Robinson J and Round D 2015. *One Treaty, One Nation.* Tross Publishing

Belgrave M 2005. Historical frictions: Maori claims and reinvented histories. Auckland University Press

Belgrave M, Kawharu M and Williams D (editors) 1989. *Waitangi Revisited: Perspectives on the Treaty of Waitangi.* Oxford University Press

Bennion T 1996. *Review of the Taranaki Report:* kaupapaptuatahi muru me te raupatu. *the muru and raupatu of the Taranaki land and people.* Waitangi Tribunal, Wai 143 and Ors. 30, April 1996. http://www.nzlii.org/nz/journals/WkoLawRw/1996/23.pdf

Benton R 1997. *The Maori language; dying or reviving?* NZCER

Bronowski J 1977. *A sense of the future.* The MIT Press.

Buck P (Te Rangi Hiroa) 1949. *The coming of the Maori.* Reprinted 1982, Whitcoulls Ltd.

Butler M 2018. *24 Years; The trials of Allan Titford.* Limestone Bluff Publishing

Byrnes G 2004. *The Waitangi Tribunal and NZ history.* Auckland: Oxford University Press

Churchman 2021. In the High Court of New Zealand, Wellington registry, CIV-2011-485-817 [2021] NZHC 1025, An application for an order recognising customary marine title and protected customary rights under The Marine and Coastal Area (Takutai Moana) Act 2011, Judgment [no. 2] of Churchman J. A PDF copy is available at https://www.courtsofnz.govt.nz/assets/5-The-Courts/high-court/high-court-lists/marine-and-coastal-area-takutai-moana-act-2011-applications-for-recognition-orders/2021-NZHC-1025_1.pdf

Department of Internal Affairs 2017. *He Whakaputanga: the Declaration of Independence 1835.* Bridget Williams Books

Doutré M undated. *Poukawa revisited ... The History Changing, Archaeological Work of Treaton Russell Price (1901 – 1986).* Posted in seven parts, starting with http://www.celticnz.co.nz/PoukawaRevisited/PoukawaPart1.html)

Doutré M, 2005. *The Littlewood Treaty: the true English text of the Treaty of Waitangi, found.* Dé Danaan Publishers

Fletcher R S 1978. *Single Track; the Construction of the Main Trunk Railway.* Auckland

Galbreath R 1998. *DSIR: making science work for New Zealand: themes from the history of the Department of Scientific and Industrial Research, 1926-1992.* Victoria University Press

Graham D 1997. *Trick or Treaty.* Institute of Policy Studies, Victoria University of Wellington

Harris E 2020. *Interrogating Ellis v The Queen: Tikanga Maori in the common law of Aotearoa New Zealand.* Maori Law Review, December 2020.

Hirschman A O 1970. *Exit voice and loyalty: responses to decline in firms, organisations and states*. Harvard University Press,
Holcroft M H 1977. *The Line of the Road*. Dunedin
Holdaway R N 1996. Arrival of rats in New Zealand. Nature 384: 225-226.
Holdaway R N 1999. A spatio-temporal model for the invasion of the New Zealand archipelago by the Pacific rat Rattus exulans. Journal of the Royal Society of New Zealand, 29:2, 91-105
Howe K 1984. *Where the waves fall*. George Allen and Unwin
Howe K R 2003. *The quest for origins*. Penguin
John Stuart Mill J S 1869. *On Liberty*. Available online: https://firstamendmentwatch.org/john-stuart-mill-liberty-1869/
Jones C 2020. *Tikanga in NZ common law*. Maori Law Review, September 2020.
Leonard B 2021 (June 7 and 10) *High Court upholds rangatiratanga in Transpower case; The precedent-setting ruling could have far-reaching effects for the way courts deal with places of significance to Maori*. Newsroom, https://www.newsroom.co.nz/high-court-upholds-rangatiratanga-in-transpower-case
Maning F E 1887. *Old New Zealand, a tale of the good old times by a pakeha Maori*. Reprinted by Golden Press 1973
Martin J E 1991 and 1998. *People, politics and power stations*. Bridget Williams Books.
McLauchlan G, King M, Keith H, Walker R and Barber L 1986. *The New Zealand book of events*. Reed Methuen Publishers
McLean J 2020a. *Parihaka: the facts*. Tross Publishing
McLean J 2020b. *Sweat and Toil; The Building of New Zealand*. Tross Publishing
McNab R 1913. *The old whaling days*. Golden Press edition, 1975

Moon B 2018. *The Rangiaowhia Incident.* 'Breaking News', NZCPR, online at https://breakingviewsnz.blogspot.com/2018/11/bruce-moon-rangiaowhia-incident.html

Ngata A 1922. *The Treaty of Waitangi,* an explanation, by The Hon. Sir Apirana Ngata MA, LLB, LitD. First published in 1922, with a translation into English by M R Jones. Published again by the Maori Purposes Fund Board with footnotes added. Available on the Victoria University website from the NZETC at http://nzetc.victoria.ac.nz/tm/scholarly/tei-NgaTrea-t1-g1-t1.html

Ngata A 1940. Speech at Waitangi, online at: http://www.ngataonga.org.nz/blog/nz-history/sir-apirana-ngatas-speech-at-the-centennial-of-the-treaty-of-waitangi-1940/

Oakley A, 2021. *The great New Zealand Treaty fraud.* Talk on YouTube available at https://www.youtube.com/watch?v=4LW2YUYv2bUandab_channel=AndyOakley, or by search under 'Andy Oakley'

Office of Treaty Settlements 1994. *Crown proposals for the settlement of Treaty of Waitangi claims.* Three booklets, "Consultation with Maori", "Detailed proposals" and "Summary"

Oliver W H 2001. *The future behind us, the Waitangi Tribunal's retrospective utopia.* In Sharp and McHugh 2001

O'Malley V 2019. *The New Zealand wars, Nga Pakanga o Aotearoa.* Bridget Williams Books

Popper K R 1959. *The logic of scientific discovery.* London.

Rata E 2021 (July 5). *Elizabeth Rata: The Road to He Puapua – Is there really a Treaty partnership?* Democracy Project, Victoria University of Wellington. https://democracyproject.nz/2021/07/05/elizabeth-rata-the-road-to-he-puapua-is-there-really-a-treaty-partnership/

Rata E 2022. *In defence of democracy. Address to the ACT Party Annual Conference.* https://www.bassettbrashandhide.com/post/professor-elizabeth-rata-in-defence-of-democracy

Robinson J L 1989. *Excess capital.* Technology Monitoring Associates

Robinson J L 2002 (June 21). *A follow-up study of the business practice survey (BPS) innovation module.* Report to the Ministry of Research Science and Technology (MoRST), unpublished.

Robinson J L 2011. *The corruption of New Zealand democracy; a Treaty industry overview.* Tross Publishing

Robinson J L 2012. *When two cultures meet; the New Zealand experience.* Tross Publishing

Robinson J L 2013. *A plague of people.* Tross Publishing

Robinson J L 2015. *Two great New Zealanders, Tamati Waka Nene and Apirana Ngata.* Tross Publishing

Robinson J L 2016. *The kingite rebellion.* Tross Publishing

Robinson J L 2019. *Dividing a nation: the return to* tikanga. Tross Publishing

Robinson J L 2020. *Unrestrained slaughter; the Maori musket wars 1800-1840.* Tross Publishing

Robinson J L 2021. *He Puapua: Blueprint for breaking up New Zealand.* Tross Publishing

Robinson J L 2021. *Hone Heke's war.* Tross Publishing

Robinson J L 2022. *The Kohimarama Conference 1860.* Tross Publishing

Robinson J L, Moon B, Round D, Butler M, Barr H and Cresswell P, 2013 and 2018 (revised edition). *Twisting the Treaty, a racial grab for wealth and power.* Tross Publishing

Royal Commission 1906. *Report and evidence of the Royal Commission on the Te Aute and Wanganui School Trusts.* AJHR (Appendices to the Journal of the House of Representatives) 1906 II G-5.

Rutherford J D. *Note on Maori casualties in their tribal wars 1801-1840.* James Rutherford papers. 1926-1963. MSS and Archives A-42, Box 16, Folder 6. Special Collections The University of Auckland Library

Schwimmer E 1966. *The world of the Maori.* Reed Education, Limpbound edition 1974

Seed P 2022. *Hoani's last stand: the real story of Rangiaowhia.* Tross Publishing

Sharp A and McHugh P G (eds) 2001. *Histories, power and loss: uses of the past, a New Zealand commentary.* Bridget Williams Books

Stavenhagen R 2005. *Report of the Special Rapporteur on the situation of human rights and fundamental freedoms of indigenous peoples, Rodolfo Stavenhagen. Addendum: Mission to New Zealand.* United Nations Economic and Social Council (online, dated 2006)

Stone R J C 2001. *From Tamaki Makaurau to Auckland.* Auckland University Press

Varesi V 2016. *The lizard strategy.* MacLehose Press

Walker R 2001. *He Tipua, the life and times of Sir Apirana Ngata.* Viking

Working Group 2019. *He Puapua: report on the working group on a plan to realise UN Declaration on the Rights of Indigenous Peoples in Aotearoa/New Zealand.* https://www.nzcpr.com/wp-content/uploads/2021/04/He-Puapua.pdf

Index

Adkin, G. L. 16-17
Apirana Ngata 7, 62-67, 70-71, 102-103, 150, 161, 197
Ardern, Jacinda 9, 137, 164, 179, 181, 200, 205, 209, 211
Aristotle 141
Bacon, Frances 115
Barr, Hugh 156
Barrett, Richard (Dicky) 82
Beaumarchais, Pierre 202
Belgrave, Michael 130, 145
Benton, Richard 161
Bolger, Jim 88
Brash, Don 155-156, 210
Browne, Gore 45. 75
Bruno, Giordano 114
Buck, Peter 18-19, 102-103, 105, 197
Busby, James 29, 32-33, 84, 189
Butler, Rev. John 24
Carman, Arthur 90
Clark, Helen 9, 170, 213, 215
Coke, Edward 194
Collins, Judith 181
Confederation of the United Tribes 29, 32, 189, 205
Cooke, Robin 132
Department of Scientific and Industrial Research (DSIR) 111-112, 115
Dieffenbach, Ernest 85
Dobson, Edward 91
Ellis, Peter 135, 172
Fenton, Francis Dart 28
Finlayson, Christopher 182, 206
Fitzroy, Robert 44-45

Galilei, Galileo 114
Gorst, John 52, 125
Graham, Doug 132-134
Grey, George 31, 44, 51-60, 75, 87, 105
Haldane principle 112-113, 115-116, 198
Hall, John 173
Hamiora Tu 49
Hector, James 110
Hemi Matini Te Nera 198
Hemi Metene Te Awaitaia 49, 198
Hobson, William 31-32, 34, 37, 59, 130, 137, 204-205
Holdaway, Richard 16
Hone Mohi Tawhia 59
Hone Waiti 49
Hongi Hika 22-24, 27, 35, 74, 83, 131, 197
Hurihanganui, Te Aniwa 150
Ironside, Rev. Samuel 42
Iwi Leaders Forum 9
Jackson, Peter 155
Jackson, Willie 165, 178-181
James, Antionette 191, 193
Jefferson, Thomas 192, 221
Jones, Carwyn 135
Karaitiana 54-56
Key, John 9, 200, 205-206, 211
King, Martin Luther 3, 163, 202
Kingi: see Wiremu Kingi
Littlewood 32-34
Love, John Agar (Jacky) 82
Luther, Martin 114
Mahuta, Nanaia 108, 164, 176, 182, 209
Mahuta, Robert 133
Maihi te Rangikakehe 59
Mandela, Nelson 202

Mao Tse Tung 159
Maori Government of Aotearoa Nu Tireni 187-188
Maori Ranger Security Division 193
Marsden, Rev. Samuel 24, 83, 95
Matene Te Whiwhi 54-55
Matike Mai Aotearoa, report 9, 168, 175
Maunsell, Rev. Robert 36
Moka 84
Moon, Bruce 130, 142, 155-156
Moriori 18-19, 22, 47
Mozart, Wolfgang Amadeus 202
Newton, Isaac 115-116
Ngata: see Apirana Ngata
O'Malley, Vincent 154
O'Regan, Tipene 133
Oliver, Bill 145-146
Orwell, George 141, 157
Paine, Tom 221
Pakira 27
Parker, David 220
Patuone 84
Pomare, Maui 103, 105
Pompallier (Bishop) 86
Price, T Russell 17
Rapata Wahawaha 62
Rata, Elisabeth 207, 216
Rewa 84
Rewi Maniapoto 7, 52-60, 94, 125, 150
Roosevelt, Franklin D. 148
Royal Society of New Zealand 110-111
Russell, Lord John 31
Rutherford, Ernest 62, 111-112
Seed, Piers 142, 153
Seymour, David 181

Smith, Percy 37
Sovereign Citizen Movement 194
Spain, Commissioner William 33, 43-44
Stavenhagen, Rodolfo 137, 166
Stubbs, George 82
Tamihana Te Rauparaha 49, 54, 191, 197
Tapsell, Phillip 83
Tawhiao 51-52, 58-60, 70, 87, 125
Te Aute College 62-63, 70, 101-103
Te Awaitaia 59, 204
Te Kooti 125
Te Puea 65, 106
Te Wake 59
Te Wharerahi 84
Te Wherowhero 29, 35-36, 38, 41-42, 51-52, 56, 74-75, 124-125, 150, 197
Thornton, John 102
Titford, Allan 172
Trotter, Chris 10
Tukihaumene 49
Turia,Tariana 143
Voltaire 159
Waitaha 17-19
Waititi, Rawiri 205
Wakaminenga government 188, 190, 193
Wakaminenga Health Council (WHC) 186-187
Wakefield, Colonel William 41
Wallace, Rev. James 42
Whitely, Rev. John 42
Wi Parata 82
Wi Tako 54-55
Wilde, Fran 203
Williams, Joe 135
Williams, Peter 223

Williams, Rev. Henry 24, 35-36
Williamson, Maurice 112
Willy, Anthony 178
Wiremu Kingi 44-46, 48, 52, 124-125
Wiremu Nero Te Awaitaia 204
Wiremu Tamihana (William Thompson) 22, 54
Woolerton, Doug 216
Yate, William 29